Empty Nest Joy

Tangible Tips for Finding Joy After Drop-off

Alexis M. Bordeaux

CONTENTS

ISBN: 979-8-9903100-5-6

www.myemptynestjoy.com

To my daughters,

you are my wildest dreams realized.

PREFACE

Your identity is not set in stone. How you answered the question, who am I? in your twenties and thirties does not have to be the same answer in your forties, fifties, and beyond.

A special letter to my empty-nest mamas

First, thank you for adding this book to your self-care regimen. While no two journeys are alike and every experience differs from person to person, I hope you will utilize the tips shared in this book and the inspiring experiences of women from across the globe as motivation and guidance when struggling with feelings of unworthiness, sadness, and immense loss. No matter where you are in your empty nest journey, whether soon-to-be empty nester, new empty nester, or seasoned empty nester, I suggest you keep a notebook or journal nearby to take notes and answer questions that may arise as you embark on this journey.

I had two thoughts while writing this book and creating the Empty Nest Joy community:

I wanted to write a book that could easily fit into your everyday bag, nestled between your favorite journal and your daily must-haves, serving as your guide and joy book. The book you pull out when life causes you to pause or challenge what you know to be true. I wanted to connect you with women who, like yourself, are attempting to relearn, expand, and embrace their, why not me, era. Women for whom life hasn't always been fair but continue to be incredibly generous. My vision was to share stories of women who have been there and done that, along with those in the beginning stages of life as empty nesters and others who wish to share tips on living an 'I did it my way' kind of life. Many of the women you will meet in this book were raised during a time when children were taught to be seen and not heard— where much was expected of them with very little guidance or consideration of their who and why. This is their story, our story. Stories of a generation of women who, after years of putting their needs on the back burner, stifling their voices, and playing it safe, are facing their fears and working through feelings of invisibility to begin the journey of redefining their life after drop-off.

No matter where you are on this journey, I hope this book will be one you reach for when in need of reaffirming nuggets and guidance for how best to navigate this season. I suggest reading all chapters, as there are nuggets in each chapter shared to help you better define and embrace your who and why. It may not feel like it now, but this will be your most transformative season, with many, many 'aha' moments. Moments where you will experience life-changing wins, along with periods of great nostalgia, causing you to pause and reflect on who you are now, who you wish to be, and how you will show up in the world.

A little bit about me:

It was in the Summer of 1993 that I wrote my first book. It has yet to be published, and to date, no eyes but my own have seen or read it. Mine was a childhood where I was taught how to survive, not how to thrive. Writing, or rather, pursuing life as a writer or anything outside of STEM (Science, Technology, Engineering, Math), was not included in my mother's survival kit for her children. As the oldest of four children, while extremely complex, my relationship with my mother remains a significant part of my who and why.

My admiration of her guts, intellect, and grace have shaped most of my decisions and played a unique role then and now in how I see myself and the world around me. I have since 1993 written two unpublished books, and if you ask those closest to me, while I chose a practical career in healthcare, writing is a central part of my who and why. But I must warn you, I have learned that I am one who discovers my thoughts through the act of writing, as I am actively writing. As you continue reading this book, you will have moments where you will say, Alexis, this is an overshare; you could have kept that tidbit to yourself.

As I attempt to complete this book for the third time, I am sitting outside a cafe on a much welcomed sunny and warm day in Amsterdam, the Netherlands. I can't help but feel honored and excited that I have the opportunity to convey a message that has become a central part of my journey to finding joy after drop-off. Looking at three open tabs on my laptop where three versions of this book exist, I have conflated them to become what is now your empty nest joy book.

Looking through a tunnel connecting the north and south sides of the Rijksmuseum, awaiting my coffee (black, two shots, with a dash of cinnamon), I can feel a bit of anxiety traveling from my chest to the inside of my right hand. Feeling pain in the center of my right hand is not new to me. Growing up and for as long as I can remember, such pain was my body's attempt at warning me that something terrible or life-altering was about to happen, and I needed to be in survival mode. Massaging the inside of my hand with my left thumb, I try to make sense of these feelings and pinpoint the cause of this new onset of pain and anxiety, but I can't for the life of me recognize what this feeling is trying to tell me.

For the most part, I've had a relatively good run here in Amsterdam, and today is an exceptionally good day. This means whatever my body is trying to warn me about has nothing to do with my current situation. Looking around the cafe, hoping my anxiety is not visible to other patrons awaiting their orders, I can feel myself beginning to breathe rather heavily through my mouth. I rub and apply even more pressure to the center of my hand, whispering 10, 9, 8, 7, 6, 5... attempting to keep calm to prevent hyperventilating. By the time I reached 3, it had become clear that I was experiencing feelings similar to those I experienced in fall of 2018 during the initial stages of writing this book.

When I began writing this book, I had a laundry list of reasons why I was unprepared and not the right person to write such a guide. I am not a formally trained writer, and while I have since 2017 nurtured a small community in my corner of the internet, writer /influencer, I am not. I found myself questioning my authority and finding reasons to support the idea that while this book is important and needed in the empty nest community, it should be written by someone more prepared, respected, and recognized.

Thoughts of being an imposter replaced common sense, forcing me to revisit events from my childhood that continue to shape my sense of self and overall view of the world. As someone who was never told I could be anything or whoever I wanted to be, I played it safe for a long time– both in my choice of career and how I present myself to the world. My definition of self was heavily influenced by a sense of lack, both real and imagined. And like many of you, my upbringing dictated my career choice and overall perception of who I am and who I am not.

For a big part of my adult life, I lived like a chameleon, morphing into whoever I needed to be to fit in and survive situations thrown at me. As I continue to look for ways to soothe my anxious mind, I run my fingers along the trackpad of my laptop, which turned on to a view of my screensaver— a picture of my two daughters at JFK airport awaiting our flight on our first trip to France. I began thinking about my path from being a married mother of two to now, a divorced empty nester navigating the many ups and downs that come with such a status. It was then that I began identifying the root of my anxieties, which led to the realization that those feelings of anxiety and imposter syndrome are due to residual trauma from constantly being asked to prove my worth and answer the most belittling question one can be asked— who do you think you are? And having to answer that question in a way that the feelings of the inquisitor are protected, while I devalue and dismiss my own humanity.

I was raised by a woman for whom everything for the family is not just a saying but an unbreakable oath. My mother, by every definition, embodies the strength, selflessness, and love that one often reads about in parenting books. If selflessness were a person, she would be my mother. From a very young age, I learned that parenting is not for the faint of heart, and the sacrifices far exceed the rewards. While I admired and appreciated how effortlessly and without a second thought she could put my needs and those of my siblings first, I vowed to use her teachings in moderation. Her actions and our many conversations on life, love, and death taught me how to care for others unselfishly and lead a life where I leave those I come across better than I found them.

While her teachings remain a central part of how I lead my life, those teachings did not light a fire in my soul as much as memories of seeing her navigate life through unspoken pain, disappointments, fears, and unrealized dreams. Those memories have fueled my desire to consistently pour into myself as much as I do my children and those I choose to love.

My approach to parenting was to ensure that my children did not only see me as a strong, all-capable superhero (in their minds) but also see the ever-evolving, flawed, and multifaceted woman who happens to be their mother. My mother's approach to parenting reaffirmed my belief that it is crucial for the development and growth of our children and the bond we create with them that they are given the opportunity to see the human side of their parents. We must connect with them beyond being their parents and allow them the opportunity to see the human side of the person they call mom. It's important that they see us as women, women who not too long ago walked in their shoes— shoes of uncertainty, fear, bewilderment, with great expectations. This belief is the driving force behind this book and the Empty Nest Joy community. Empty Nest Joy was created to help parents like yourself prepare to navigate life as soon-to-be empty nesters, new empty nesters, and those still trying to define and maintain joy as seasoned empty

nesters. If you embrace it, your empty nest years can be your most transformative years yet.

But I would be naïve and disingenuous to say it will be easy. This new season and transition into life as an empty nester comes with many ups and downs, where your emotions are all over the place. There will be moments of fear, uncertainty, anxiety, and immense nostalgia, but I can assure you, while there is much to learn and periods of painful growth, there is, after all is said and done, great contentment and joy after drop-off. No matter where you are in your empty nest journey, I hope the tips shared in this book are added to your self-care regimen, helping you to bring back, add, and maintain a bit more joy in your life. May you include it in your strategies for thriving in what is the most redefining season of your life.

As you begin this journey and move forward with identifying who you are now, who you would like to be moving forward, and what you would like this next season to look like, remember this: you may receive pushback from friends and family who will have difficulty accepting your quest for change and growth, but don't let that stop you; remain focused on silencing both internal voices and those of people who will try to convince you to leave well enough alone. There will be moments where inner voices and voices of those around you will attempt to remind you of your lack, your age, and your past, giving you a laundry list of reasons why you should remain comfortable in the familiar, as your best years are well behind you. Deciding to break away from the norm and pave your own way may provoke discomfort and insecurity among those closest to you. It may not feel like it, but we all are put into boxes by our family, friends, and society. Boxes that are created to keep us malleable and predictable. Many in your circle will find it hard to accept your quest for an expanded worldview and thirst for purposeful experiences, but stay focused and remember your why. Their discomfort will soon turn to curiosity, leading them to find the courage to explore the possibility of new experiences and dream new dreams. Keep moving forward, even if those naysayers are empty nesters like yourself.

I've learned there are three types of empty-nesters navigating this season of transformation:

Most common are those who believe life has passed them by and are left with few options or opportunities for new experiences. The idea of joy after drop-off is not only foreign but seems like a pipe dream, as the belief that their best years are behind them is much more plausible than the possibility of having new experiences

and realizing new dreams. They have accepted the idea that their role as full-time parents was, and will forever be, the all of them. They have great difficulty unlearning what was taught to them about this stage of life and move with extreme caution, doubt, and self-created limitations.

The second type is the optimist; they move as if a new world has opened up for them, offering new possibilities, experiences, friendships, and love. Their motto is, "There is no time like the present." They are open to all possibilities and take chances deemed unrealistic and out of character for a person of a certain age, race, and background. When faced with failure, uncertainty, and periods of loneliness, they find courage in the belief that opportunity does, indeed, favor the bold.

The third and last are those who are indifferent. They are unsure of what to expect in this stage and don't spend much time dwelling on the past, or future for that matter. They go with the flow and are open to whatever life throws at them; they are the poster child for people who can easily go with the flow. Good or bad, they roll with the punches with a one-day-at-a-time approach.

No matter which category you fall into, I invite you to fully embrace the possibility of new beginnings and remain open to receiving the tips and inspirational stories in this book. There is great beauty in this empty nest journey. Whether prepared or not, every parent (if they are lucky) will one day join this club and be faced with a question that I hope to help you answer:

The children have left to pave their own way; where do I go from here?

We live in a society where the word purpose is used to explain a path that is supposed to be the end-all, be-all. There is this unspoken rule that once you've found your calling, your 'thing,' that thing should be the all of you...forever. But fortunately, or unfortunately, depending on who you ask, purpose is not finite. You don't just find it and stay there. As you continue to change and grow, so will your purpose, dreams, and expectations, which is perfectly okay. Accepting and embracing the idea of situational purpose is a vital part of this journey. Whether redefining career objectives, adapting to your now "empty nest," or addressing health and wellness concerns, situational purpose provides the freedom needed to reassess and realign life

goals according to the unique demands of this season.

Embracing situational purpose implies recognizing that goals and motivations will change, and what was once the foundation of our "why" may remain part of our next chapter but will not be the all of it. It encourages a mindset that values adaptability and resourcefulness, acknowledging that different situations may require different sets of priorities or objectives. It gives room to change our minds, removing and adding those things that may or may not fit our definition of a well-lived life.

To my single mamas, breathe!

The anxiety, uncertainty, and feelings of immense loss can feel suffocating, but trust me, you will get through this. Whether you are a soon-to-be empty nester or a new empty nester, asking, where did the time go? I can assure you there is a large community of women asking the same exact question, wondering what happens now and where they go from here. I encourage you to use this time to prepare yourself mentally and physically to experience every opportunity that will present itself to you this season. You are just getting started— stay prepared! If you let it, this can be your season of immense growth, where you experience life-changing opportunities, opportunities society would like you to believe are reserved for the "young."

If you're a soon-to-be empty nester, use this last year as an intro to your year of, why not: why not you - why not now? Being a single empty nester is not, will not, be easy— especially if your entire world was centered (raising both hands and feet) around your child(ren). But I can assure you, joy abounds after drop-off. If you remain open to learning new ways of redefining what empty nesting means to you, you will thrive in this season and inspire others to walk with full certainty that their best years are not behind them.

To mamas going through separation and/or divorce, may you find solace and clarity from the tips and stories shared in this book, and may you always remember that you are not alone. I've been where you are and know firsthand the challenges and uncertainties associated with juggling motherhood while navigating what may be one of the most challenging times of your life. You are not a failure. Being a divorced woman is not the all of you and will not be the end of your life or love story. I want to fast-forward to your future self, where you will stand stronger, with more insight into self, love, and what (by your definition) brings you joy. Trust me,

friend, you will get through this. You will make it to the other side. You will find peace, comfort, clarity, and, dare I say, joy again.

To seasoned empty nesters still trying to find your way, it is not too late. You are not useless or without purpose. No matter how long it's been since the children left to pave their own way, no matter how long you've been trying to understand this journey and answer what's next. Who am I? and where do I go from here? I write these words not as a pacifier for your tears, disappointment, frustration, and doubt but to encourage you to continue your search, tweak as needed, reassess your position and the role you play in the ups and downs of your life, and push yourself to take up space in your skin and your corner of the world. Your experiences matter— your expertise matters. Your desire to feel more, experience more, and live boldly and out loud is not unrealistic or unattainable; keep pushing forward. You have so much to offer the world, and your best days are certainly not behind you. Society will tell you that life after drop-off is the prerequisite for life as the invisible woman; I can assure you that nothing is further from the truth. No matter where you are at this stage, no matter your understanding of what this time in your life should look like, I encourage you to not only keep an open mind but remain open to unlearning everything taught to you about life after drop-off and prepare to take up space and thrive in your season of, why not now and why not me.

Lastly, I raise a glass to all women over 50 trying to find peace and acceptance of their aging bodies in a world that thrives on your (perceived) insecurities. You are not invisible. Your worth, desirability, and joy are not tied to your ability to uphold unrealistic beauty standards to appear forever twenty-five; you are enough— changing bodies, hot flashes, mood swings, and all.

Now grab a cup of tea, coffee, or wine, and let's get into the business of finding joy after drop-off.

Alexis M. Bordeaux - Empty Nest Joy

"And by the way, everything in life is writable about if you have the outgoing guts to do it, and the imagination to improvise. The worst enemy to creativity is self-doubt." —Sylvia Plath

PART ONE

Soon-to-be Empty Nester

Why Change Can Feel Crippling

"The butterfly said to the sun, 'They can't stop talking about my transformation. I can only do it once in my lifetime. If only they knew they can do it at any time and in countless ways." — *Dodinsky*

June 27, 2013 — Graduation Day — Brooklyn, New York

I remember my daughter's last year of high school as if it were yesterday. She, of course, was elated; this was the beginning of what she called her best year yet. If you asked her about this time in her life, she would say, "I've waited my whole life for senior year of high school." The last year of high school ushers the end of her high school career, with graduation signaling the start of new beginnings, where late morning starts and freedom, lots and lots of freedom, are synonymous with autonomy and self-discovery. I know we hear and say it often, and it can seem a bit cliche, but time waits for no one, and boy, do they grow up fast. One day you're changing poopy diapers, running after a temperamental two-year-old, and before you know it, you find yourself juggling time between volleyball and track practice. You then blink for a minute, and there you are, taking pictures at their prom and high school graduation. My youngest daughter is a social butterfly who believes it is her life's work to participate in as many activities as time allows. This means I can confidently include private chauffeur as a perfected skill set. Her junior year of high school was a milestone year filled with activities and a mile-long list of must-dos in preparation for the final chapter of her high school career.

Like all milestone years, it ended just as fast as it came, and she could not wait to begin her last and final year of high school. While she was ecstatic to participate in all things senior year-related, all I could think about and look forward to was the fact that this would be my last year dropping and picking her up from that dreadful drop-off/pick-up line. That year was one of the busiest years of my parenting life. Emotions were all over the place, and I was mentally and physically stretched in every possible direction. This was not my first ride at the rodeo, as my oldest daughter is twenty-five and a college graduate, but it was my last, and my heart could not handle it.

As parents, we take great pride in preparing our children for life after high school. We strive to provide them with tools that will enable them to take care of themselves, with or without us, while reminding them to slow down and enjoy all that youth has to offer before jumping head-first into adulthood. We talk, guide, and pray that they will take lessons learned at home to help shape their who and why and navigate the many ups and downs of young adulthood, but we, unknowingly, fail to prepare ourselves for what is the most transformative years of our own lives. Inculcating values to smooth their journey and equip them for the tumultuous ride of young adulthood, we forget that we, too, will be going through a transition that, if not prepared, can cause great sadness and anxiety that can easily be heightened by the roller coaster of emotions and self-doubt that comes with life as an empty-nester.

Looking back, I wish I had taken the early stages of empty nesting more seriously. I wish I made a conscious decision to better prepare myself during my daughter's last year of high school for my second act, my life after drop-off. Like many of you, my daughter's last year of high school was one where the focus was primarily on her— her needs, her future, and making sure she enjoyed her last year, all while preparing her for college. I enjoyed every bit of it(drop-off/pick-up line excluded). I am a girl mom. I love every bit of parenting girls.

But I am the first to admit that in the midst of raising young ladies who would one day become confident, self-sufficient, responsible young women, I forgot that I, too, need some tender loving care. I, too, must prepare myself to be on my own, with much more time to think and just be. The idea alone gave me great anxiety. As parents, we raise our children to know who they are without us; we now need to figure out who we are without them.

While I knew some preparation was needed to navigate this next season of my life, I had expansive dreams, very specific goals, and a mile-long bucket list of must-dos to start with; I was unclear about the "who" part of this journey. Who I needed to become to live my definition of a well-lived life. And answer the question, who am I outside of mom and caretaker? Child-rearing is no walk in the park. I took parenting pretty seriously, dedicating most of my time and a considerable chunk of my life to doing my best at parenting children who, hopefully, will not be walking billboards of unhealed childhood pain and trauma.

Part of that was learning to differentiate situations, people, places, and things that are supposed to be permanent parts of my life versus those that are here for a season. I know firsthand the challenges associated with moving on and accepting a new chapter. The fear associated with starting anew can be crippling, making it easy to get stuck in the familiar. Most people will never reach their full potential or become who they wish to be, not due to lack of opportunity or ingenuity, but being too attached to who they've always been and determined to do things as they've always been done. Familiarity is the prerequisite for stagnation and a life of, should have, and could have.

I became a single parent through divorce during my oldest daughter's junior year of high school. Divorce not only changed my self-perception, but it also changed my parenting style. I became the parent who overextended herself, overcompensating for the physical and emotional loss of a second parent. My focus and priorities were solely on the needs and health of my daughters, with very little thought on what life would look like for me once they were out of the nest.

I had some ideas and even spent some time jotting down activities and hobbies I would like to take on after drop-off, but like many of you, my identity was tied to my role as mom. Who am I? What do I want out of life now? Now that time is on my side, what does empty-nesting mean to me? Those, along with questions about the many phases of aging, are questions I, for a while, struggled to answer. Those are the questions I hope to help you answer as you continue this journey. What is empty nesting, and what should it look like for you right now and in the future?

It is no secret that we as a society have a love/hate relationship with aging. Ageism is rooted in a cultural belief that aging is all negative. We've convinced ourselves that it is bad to age, so it's best not to bring it up or only bring it up when complaining about its challenges. So, it's not surprising that when we think about those life changes associated with aging, like being an empty nester, conversations around that stage of life are either depressing or an afterthought.

The word "empty nest" comes from the family life cycle theory, where the empty nest stage is the seventh and final stage of the cycle. It involves children leaving home, and parents left to learn how to navigate this new stage of life, sometimes alone. There is a finality about dropping your child off at college or when they move out on their own that forces parents to accept that they are closing the door on one of the most celebrated seasons of their lives, to enter a season that is not only less celebrated, but filled with negative expectations and immense feelings of loss that can lead to empty nest syndrome.

Empty nest syndrome refers to the grief many parents feel when their children leave the nest. Typically, this is more common in women, as they are more likely to have had the role of primary caregiver. You will find that women who are full-time parents are more often affected than women who also work outside the home. A lot has changed since the idea of empty nest syndrome first surfaced. With more mothers now working outside the home, giving them a role beyond that of a caregiver, being an empty nester is not the death sentence it once was.

Now more than ever, empty nesters are realizing that this season is an opportunity to reinvent themselves without needing permission, validation, or elaborate explanation of their why. It is a season where your wants and needs are prioritized, taking center stage in your overall why. That kind of realization can be both freeing and exciting, yet extremely intimidating, especially if most of your time prior to being an empty nester was spent with your children— doing what they enjoy, participating in their activities, and playing chauffeur. Throw in the belief that your value and goodness are tied to your ability to care for others; time alone, focusing on your needs can feel selfish and overindulgent. Time was one of my most feared privileges. Time, especially when experienced alone, forces us to answer those pesky questions that can easily be avoided during our busy child-rearing years. Questions to keep in mind as you navigate this new season.

Who am I outside of being a mom?
What are some things I enjoy doing alone?

How will I honor this season?

What does an empty nest life look like for me?

And where do I begin?

I encourage you to take note of the suggestions in this book. They will help you answer these questions and better prepare for your empty nest years now, while your child is in high school.

But first, congratulations, you're almost at the finish line! If you're like thousands of parents around the world, you are now experiencing what I call The Five Stages of Accepting Life as an Empty nester.

The Five Stages of Accepting Life as an Empty-nester

Stage one:

Joy— Elated at the thought of getting your life back and your time back and redefining yourself on your terms. As you know, being a mother is only one aspect of your identity. And no matter how much you enjoyed life as a full-time mom, there is a part of you waiting in anticipation of what could be. You feel little to no shame or guilt about your excitement of what could be. You may not know where to start or what your empty nest life should look like; you're apprehensive yet extremely excited.

Stage two:

Planning—You've started planning your new life, looking at all possibilities, re-visiting old dreams and hobbies that didn't quite fit into your life as a full-time parent, contemplating what could be, and jotting down ideas of hobbies and activities you would like to rediscover and learn. The idea that this will be your fresh start, a blank page in your next chapter, can be both exhilarating and daunting.

Stage three:

Nostalgia— Where did the time go? If only I could return to the old days when things were simpler, comfortable, planned, and predictable. There is something to be said about having a familiar routine. It is comfortable, predictable, and, well, familiar. This stage is by far the most frightening. Thoughts of what used to be can be paralyzing. Memory distortion is at an all-time high during this stage.

No matter how good or bad the old days were, we tend to find comfort and appreciate those familiar things as they are usually predictable, comfortable, and don't require much change of thought, routine, or habit. Nostalgia will have you glamorizing those things that you know deep down are not working for you or you've outgrown but find comfort in because they are familiar.

Stage four:

Fear— Did I do enough? Did I provide them with a proper foundation and cushion to ensure their path is easier than mine was at their age? What if I didn't? What if, what if, what-ifs run amok. Senior year is very similar to sitting at a gate in an airport thinking about the luggage you packed the night before, wondering if you packed everything— do I have all I need for this long haul? What have I missed? You know there's little you can do at this point, but anxiety and fear are suffocating, feeding into your fear of being ill-prepared and not having done enough.

Stage five:

Excitement/Acceptance— Realizing good, bad, or indifferent, you did your best, and focus on not letting fear, dressed as concern, keep you from being present to experience fully one of the many milestones you will share with your child(ren).

I was stuck between three and four for what seemed like forever. For the life of me, I could not get over how quickly time had passed. Followed by days where I feared that I had not done enough, said enough, or prepared them well enough for life's ups and downs. Don't get me wrong, motherhood was never about raising perfect children, as how can I raise someone to be something I, myself, will never be. My role was to ensure that when it's all said and done, if and when my daughters are asked to tell their stories, they will have the courage, insight, and grace to appoint themselves as the main character of their life story.

Their story should always resemble who they are, not who I want them to be or act like. My focus was to ensure that no matter where they are in the world, they wouldn't be walking billboards highlighting my pain, failures, and shortcomings. While our past should never dictate who and what we become, untreated wounds can take root, grow, and manifest in ways that can negatively alter the trajectory of our lives and that of future generations. Boy, am I grateful for therapy!

Once I reached the fifth and final stage, I went back to number two, planning. I began searching for online groups and platforms dedicated to women entering or thriving in their empty nest years. The results were few, which begged the question, have other empty nesters not experienced this void? And if they have, how have they prepared themselves for life after drop-off? After months of online and offline research, I began compiling tips and tricks that have become integral parts of my ability to navigate this new season successfully.

I've had many failed projects, ventures, and more 'aha' moments than I care to share. Some lessons have left lasting impressions, while others are mere afterthoughts. But it is those that have been tried and found to be true that I've added in this book to ensure your transformation starts early and bears fruit that you didn't think was possible.

Whether dropping them off at university, a new apartment, or military service... is there happiness after drop-off? Absolutely. But happiness comes and goes, while joy is not dependent on time, place, or feeling. When happiness eludes you, joy will maintain you till the end. But like anything life-changing, preparation is key. I hope the tips written in this book will help you better prepare to navigate this new chapter of your life, from soup to nuts.

Five tips for preparing for life as an empty nester while your child is in their last year of high school

One-
If you haven't already included journaling into your self-care regimen, I recommend buying a journal and follow these writing tips:

Your first page and all pages following your first entry should include the date and answer to this question: How am I feeling today? Keep in mind that feelings are not permanent and, most times, do not reflect your reality. Give yourself the grace to feel all feelings to determine better who and what brings them on and what, if anything, you do to help them run their course. Don't feel obligated to act on every feeling or mood. Preparing for life as an empty nester is like preparing for life with a new partner; grace, kindness, and self-awareness are paramount. Keeping an open mind and showing compassion and grace to yourself, as you would a loved one, is key to thriving in your empty nest life.

Move with kindness; self-compassion should be a central part of your day-to-day regimen, especially when consumed with feelings of loss and unworthiness. Sometimes, doing nothing but journaling your feelings is all that is needed to help you move forward. Seeing your candid thoughts on paper is both powerful and liberating. Don't journal with hopes of finding answers or fixing a problem; that's not what journaling is for. We don't journal to find answers; we journal to provide ourselves a safe space to express our thoughts and feelings without fear and shame, devoid of the need to appear like we have it all together.

The first entry should describe as detailed as possible: what does being an empty-nester mean to me? Move away from obvious definitions and speak from your heart. Does it mean freedom? Opportunity for new beginnings and experiences? Does it make you feel old, without value or purpose? Afraid of the unknown? Perhaps overwhelmed? Lost? Indifferent? Be honest with yourself; this is your safe space.

Once you've answered those questions, move on to answering what your empty nest life will look like. Be as over-the-top and specific as possible. Make sure to pull from your idea of best-case scenarios and not that of your parents or women who came before you. Be elaborate with your wants. What would you do today if you knew you wouldn't fail? Let journaling serve as your secret place— a place where you share your daily happenings, dreams, goals, and aspirations. End each journal entry with three words/sentences of affirmations, such as:

1   I am not too old, and it's not too late.
2   I am wonderfully made; my experiences are valuable and have prepared me for this season.
3   I have everything I need within me to create the life I desire and deserve.
4   I was made for this— joy, peace, love, and opportunity surround me.
5   I lack nothing; my cup overflows. I have the capacity and ability to be part of the change I wish to see in the world.

You don't have to journal daily, although daily journaling can be an effective stress reducer and can help you maintain a clear and clutter-free mind. Journal as often as needed, making journaling a welcome addition to your "me time."

Two-
Get into the habit of doing things that do not include your child(ren). By far, the last year of high school is the most stressful time for both parent and child. As parents, it's easy to put our social life on hold to ensure all I's and T's are dotted and crossed. It's easy to make their activities our activities, from test preparation, college tours, school dances, and everything in between. The last year is not only the most stressful time of the high school experience; it's also the year when days move at lightning speed. One minute, you're dropping them off at homecoming, you blink, and you're at Target shopping for dorm must-haves.

This is why, speaking from experience, with a lot of would've, could've, and should've under my belt, I suggest exploring new hobbies and making time to do those things that bring you joy and add value to your day now. As you plan their day and rearrange your schedule to be available for their activities, leave room for some "me time" hobbies. This is the perfect time to re-acquaint yourself with hobbies you've not had time to enjoy and take on new hobbies outside your comfort zone.

This should also be included in your journaling sessions, answering the question: How do I feel when doing things without your child(ren)? Do you feel guilty, happy, regretful? The first two months of doing activities that didn't include my daughters were tough. I found myself experiencing a significant amount of guilt when engaging in activities that didn't include them. Jotting down those feelings and making it a point to understand the reason behind those feelings helped me realize how much of an influence my mother's sacrificial lamb-type parenting style had on me.

To this very day, my mother finds great joy in sharing how she sacrificed herself and her time for the greater good, which, in her case, was her children. In her eyes and mine, parenting by sacrifice was a sign of a good parent. She took great pride in sharing the sacrifices she's made for the benefit and well-being of her children; I found myself doing the same. It wasn't until I started engaging in hobbies that didn't include my girls that I realized, not all sacrifices are created equal. Some are done for the betterment of our families, while others are out of codependency and fear. It became evident that those feelings of guilt and regret stemmed from the idea that taking care of myself is selfish and that I am putting my needs above my children, an idea that's not only false but a grave misunderstanding of my role as a parent.

Including those episodes of guilt and growth in my daily journaling sessions helped me put a name to those feelings and understand their origin, opening the door for healing and the creation of healthy habits. There is nothing wrong with having a social life or participating in activities that do not include your children. You do not win the "Best Parent of the Year" award for not making time for yourself or relying on your children to be your only source of entertainment. Having a social life will help them understand the importance of self-care. It fosters an environment where your children and partner understand your need for social interactions that are not tied to your role as mom/wife/ caretaker.

Three-
Stay in contact with old friends and be open to making new ones. I can't stress enough the importance of having a solid tribe prior to your life as an empty nester. Making friends after forty-five, while not impossible, is no easy feat. By age forty-five, most people have friendships spanning fifteen to twenty years, and are pretty set and comfortable with their circle of friends, and see no reason to add new people into their girl gang. Create a schedule that includes monthly sister-friend time. Time

when you spend a couple of hours (face-to-face) bonding and nurturing current friendships.

Don't shy away from reaching out to old friends who, like you, are so bombarded with parenting and life's ups and downs that they forget to feed the carefree person within them, yearning for conversations that don't include PTA meetings and college prep classes. When it comes to friendships, never assume that no news is good news. Parenting is one of the most demanding jobs in the world; an absentee friend doesn't necessarily mean a bad friend. More often than not, an absentee friend is a person so consumed with ensuring the well-being of others that their needs never make it to their to-do list.

While making friends after forty-five is not easy, I am happy to report that due to the power and reach of the internet, I have met some incredible women who I am thrilled to call friends, some sister-friends, even. The great thing about the internet, specifically social media, is the ability to connect with people from all over the globe who share your interests and have similar backgrounds and belief systems. The probability of finding like-minded individuals looking to meet new people to add to their circle of friends is high and in your favor. Don't shy away from Facebook groups. Facebook groups can be your bridge to finding like-minded people on similar journeys. There is a group for everyone and everything. I remember not too long ago being added to a Facebook group specifically for women who love bearded men. I am unsure how or who added me, but every now and again, the social media gods show favor over my beard-loving heart, and for that, I am eternally grateful.

As I write this, I can hear those closest to me screaming, "But you have only three, maybe four close friends!" and they are correct. Now more than ever, it is extremely important to take great care in how you curate your friend group. Not everyone will understand your need for re-invention of self and may project their fears and misunderstanding of what this season should and shouldn't look like on you. You must determine early people who should be at the front row of your life versus those who should be kept in nosebleed. When it comes to close friendships, more doesn't necessarily mean best. Don't isolate yourself or live as the lone woman on the island, but choose your triangle wisely.

.

Four -
Be open to reinventing yourself. There is no one way to do life. One of the biggest challenges in fully grasping the idea of being able to reinvent oneself is believing that life is one size fits all, and any deviation from what is expected and deemed normal makes one weird (as if being weird is the worst thing one could be). Happy is

the woman who navigates life unafraid of being labeled -weird, wild, risky, different...and content is the woman who takes full advantage of her right to change her mind, shake things up, and hit them with an occasional plot twist.

As simple as that sounds, unlearning what was taught to you as criteria for a well-lived life can be the hardest challenge to overcome. Especially when it comes to identifying who you are and who you are not. That kind of clarity will play a significant role in how well you are able to take full advantage of life-changing opportunities presented to you on this journey. This will position you to astutely determine opportunities and situations that are in alignment with your vision for this stage of your life versus those that do not speak to who you are and where you wish to go. Understanding that you don't have to *insert myopic social norms *, live up to, fit into, make excuses for, or settle for anything outside of your idea of a well-lived life and move with the understanding that there is no one way to do life, is key to navigating this season of your life.

The best gift you can give yourself during this season is to adopt the golden rule that life begins where societal acceptance and validation end. The desire to reinvent oneself does not have an expiration date. Challenging false assumptions about your capabilities once your children have left the nest exposes the many myths around aging and opens doors to new experiences and opportunities. Reinvention of self embraces the mindset that life is a dynamic and ever-changing journey. Adopting a more proactive approach positions you to navigate challenges better, pursue aspirations, and shape your destiny on your terms. Where you don't live life from the standpoint of "that's just the way things are," which can be a limiting perspective that undermines your potential for personal growth and meaningful experiences, but view each experience as an opportunity for growth and explore ways for living a life that goes beyond what is expected of you for a person your age, or background.

When we believe and live a life of, that's just the way things are, we take on a coat of helplessness. We believe we have reached our peak and have exhausted our most fruitful years. We accept that there are limitations that are determined by our age and our ability to care for others that cannot be overcome. Creating your Empty Nest Joy is about challenging outdated assumptions, exposing and pushing through limiting beliefs to eventually live a life where you are the author of your story.

What does it mean to reinvent oneself? Is it a sign that something is wrong with this current version of yourself? Does it mean you've been holding back or stifling your potential? Is the desire to reinvent oneself a sign of a midlife crisis? No. No. No! Being open to, or seeking to reinvent oneself, put simply, is giving yourself permission and space to grow and experience new relationships, possibilities, and new ways of thinking and living on your terms.

It means moving away from the idea that your best days are behind you, as you have done and experienced everything life has to offer. It is allowing yourself the freedom to go with the flow and rest on the knowledge that you have everything you need to enter this new season and thrive. It's an understanding that an empty nest does not equate to an empty life, and you can be many things and experience many joys that are not determined by age, financial status, or outward appearance.

Four questions to answer when thinking about reinventing yourself in this season:

- How do you feel about this new season?
- Who in your life inspires you to live outside societal boundaries associated with aging?
- One thing I put aside during the rearing of my child(ren) that I will do within six months of life as an empty nester.
- Top three things I would like to do within my first year as an empty nester.

Notice the focus is on you, your wants, feelings, interpretation, and expectations. Prepare for this season by paying attention to your wants and needs. Make a conscious decision to push away thoughts and claims that focusing on yourself is selfish. Planning must be based on your interpretation of empty nest joy. Often, when faced with a life-altering change or decision, we naturally refer to the experiences and recommendations of those who came before us, and while we can all appreciate and find value in the parenting style of women from past generations, I don't believe parenting and life as an empty nester is one size fits all. What may have been an ideal and well-lived life for your mother and grandmother may not work for you and your vision for your empty nest years.

Give yourself permission to dream and visualize your 'best' empty nest life. Take note of what speaks to you when thinking about what that life will look like. Remember, empty nest joy is subjective. It differs from person to person. Your empty nest joy may be the happiness you feel when finally able to sleep past eight AM on Saturday mornings. It could mean buying an RV for quick weekend trips or long-distance travel. It could also mean volunteering at your local hospital or medical center…your nest, your choice.

You have the right to add and subtract as you see fit. Most importantly, you can, at any moment, change your mind and throw a couple of plot twists in there, too. Get creative. Get excited. Think back to your younger days of planning how you would raise your child(ren), the steps you said you would take to ensure they have all they need for a happy and joyful childhood. While all your plans may not have panned out as you hoped, you did your best and now have the opportunity to plan the next equally important season of your life.

This is not the time to simply go with the flow. Be intentional with your dreams so they can turn into visions that lead to your reality. Enjoy this last year of full-time mommy to your child(ren), but don't neglect your dreams. Rise to the occasion and be present. Empty nesting is a privilege. Seeing your child(ren) grow to no longer needing you around the clock is a gift. Receive it as such, and prepare yourself for the journey of finding and building your empty nest joy. Remember, you do not need permission to reinvent yourself, an idea that can simultaneously feel liberating and frightening. When we think about reinventing ourselves or starting over, we often think of changes that require months, sometimes years, of planning and preparation. We may also worry about how those around us will receive said change. While those feelings are normal and more common than you might think, they should not be your norm or become part of your criteria when deciding whether or not it's time for a change.

First, your desire for change or reinvention of self doesn't require grand announcements, doesn't have to be a huge production, and most certainly does not require approval from others. Starting over can be as simple as saying, today, I resolve to control how I spend my time, who I allow access to my space, and how I react to outside stimuli. While deciding on the things you would like to change during the next few years, keep in mind that you can't be everything to everyone and still be true to yourself. And you can't be true to yourself if you have not yet fully developed your who, what, why, and how.

Who are you, as defined by you?
What would you like this next season to look like?
Why is this time in my life important for future plans?
How will I show up in the world?

Five -
We are in this together. I can't speak enough about the importance of building and establishing solid relationships without mentioning how vital it is to stay connected and transparent with your life partner. When going through the roller coaster of feelings associated

with going from full-time parent to an empty nester, fight the urge to isolate yourself and your feelings from your partner. If anyone can relate with what you're feeling and experiencing, it's them. Talk it out, and share your fears, sadness, and plans. Whatever you do, do not exclude them from this chapter; share this experience - good, bad, or indifferent. They deserve to see that part of you and share in your rediscovery of self. Truth is, they may not say it aloud, but they, too, are scared and grieving the end of this chapter. Talk it out! It wasn't until conducting research for this book that I learned how high the probability of divorce is during the last year of high school and after drop-off, which I will share later in the book. But I feel it is important to speak directly with soon-to-be empty nesters, as I can't stress enough the importance of making a conscious decision to include your partner in navigating your feelings of loss and uncertainty, now, at the beginning of this journey. While creating your personal 'me time' routine, be sure to add some 'we time' in there, too. Time that you dedicate to spending quality time with your partner, not just sharing your worries, fears, and feelings of loss, but including them in your dreams and future plans.

Parenting is a full-time job. It's easy to think that time spent with your children and spouse doing family activities equates to quality time with your hubby/wife. We tend to settle into a routine where the needs of our children take center stage, forgetting the romantic side of our relationships/marriages. For many couples, it's not until the children are off to college that they realize the children were the glue of the relationship and a big part of their entertainment. As you move forward this season, making time to re-acquaint yourself with your partner will make a world of difference. The bond created during this season will help ease the transition into the next phase of parenting; now more than ever, mutual support and understanding are vital. You are entering uncharted grounds, where you will experience a myriad of emotions and explore thought processes that may be out of character; mutual compassion must take center stage to create a safe space where you and your partner can freely express yourself without judgment and shame. You'll be much more aware of each other's wants, nuances, and needs now, during your child's last year of high school, and well into your empty nest years.

As you gain more time for yourself, you also gain more time with your partner, which can be good or challenging, depending on your situation. Going on this journey as a team will offer the opportunity to experience this season knowing, good, bad, or other, you have someone who is fully in sync with your feelings, who, through open and honest conversations, will help you connect the dots and find strength in knowing you are not alone on this empty nest journey.

Whether single, married, or it's complicated, a self-care plan is an absolute must during this season. Years ago, when traveling for work, I made it a point to always book a spa day and note the closest park, museum, or art gallery to ensure I had some 'me time' that didn't center around work or preparation for the next day. This ritual continues to be a significant part of my self-care routine, ensuring that no matter where I am, I prioritize time to recenter and engage in activities pleasing to my soul.

If you don't have a self-care plan or regimen, bookmark this now and create one after completing this book. Your self-care plan should include activities like daily walks to nowhere, playing tourist in your city, and moments of stillness that are not production-centered or filled with busy work. This last year will go by in a flash; you will experience many ups and downs, but believe me when I say you are about to enter your most fruitful season yet. Stay encouraged, and allow yourself the freedom and grace to go through all emotions. No matter what is thrown at you during this season or feelings of unworthiness, nostalgia, and loss that will come to remind you of the good old days do not shrink!

Do not subscribe to the idea that your best years are behind you— they are not; you are just getting started.

Answer these questions in your next journal entry:

- Think back to a time when you faced a significant change; what was your most impactful plan of action?

- What societal pressures cause you to fear this period in your life?

- Who do you turn to when feeling nostalgic and/or overwhelmed about this season?

- What song perfectly describes your current attitude about this stage?

- It is the Summer of your high school graduation; what would you tell your younger self about the future?

"My only advice is to stay aware, listen carefully, and yell for help if you need it."
—Judy Blume

Learning to Embrace Stillness Can Change Your Life

"Live in each season as it passes; breathe the air, drink the drink, taste the fruit, and resign yourself to the influence of the earth." — Henry David Thoreau

May 16, 2016 — Going down memory lane — Brooklyn, NY

I remember a conversation with a girlfriend in the beginning stages of planning her second act, her next move once her daughter left for University. Catherine was experiencing an immense sense of loss and nostalgia and was overwhelmed with the idea that her daughter would no longer need her. She felt she had to put up a front, pretend to be at ease with the coming changes, go with the flow, and not make a big fuss about these milestones since, like many others, they are expected parts of parenting.

You see, my friend is a fixer. She is one who sees a problem, and immediately, the wheels of getting to the other side of "problem solved" begins to turn in her head. When it came to the changes awaiting her, her approach was to fix first and feel later, an approach she learned from her father. So, it wasn't surprising to see her jump into planning mode when her daughter began her senior year of high school. She began planning ways to fill her soon-to-be empty nest and not make a fuss about her feelings of loss and apprehension of becoming an empty nester. She felt voicing that such a void existed could be interpreted as unstable, indicative of someone who had created an unhealthy bond with her child, an idea I understood all too well.

There is this unspoken rule that once a child turns eighteen and leaves for University or takes other paths, they are grown and should be treated as such. It is as if they have somehow, overnight, gained profound wisdom and understanding of life and self that replaces the support and anchor role found in a present and devoted parent, and parents must accept this idea unquestioningly to avoid appearing unstable and lacking boundaries.

I remember my friend asking, "Well, Alexis, what now? What do I do now?" Her need for answers on her next steps was palpable. Her voice had a sense of urgency that begged for answers so she could immediately jump into planning and take action. She was faced with two very familiar problems: overcoming feelings of fear, loneliness, and purposelessness that often come with life as a new empty nester. And two, an urgency to devise a plan filled with activities that would keep her busy and on the move to avoid appearing like someone with a distorted sense of self and an unhealthy idea of the parent/child relationship.

I understood her need for answers, immediate fillers, and a road map. With all its ups and downs, child-rearing is the one experience, the only experience, where your position and contributions are everlasting. One doesn't become an ex-parent or the artist formerly known as mom/dad once the children have left the nest. Going from being needed almost regularly to sometimes, maybe, can take some getting used to. Having clarity on what life after drop-off should look like is not something that happens overnight. It is not something to rush to but something to go through while providing yourself the grace and space to experience stillness as a grounding force, allowing you to pause, reflect, and gain much-needed perspective.

In the midst of change, embracing moments of stillness cultivates resilience, fostering a sense of inner peace that acts as an anchor during the turbulence of transition. It grants the opportunity to assess one's values, aspirations, and fears, aiding in making more informed decisions rather than succumbing to impulsive reactions. Mindfulness, honed through stillness, facilitates the appreciation of the present moment, helping us make decisions based on facts versus those based on fear, lack, and experiences that no longer serve us.

In May 2016, during a trip to New York, I decided to visit my childhood neighborhood of Brooklyn, something I hadn't done in years. Walking down the familiar mixture of brownstone houses and six-story buildings that lined the block, a bittersweet nostalgia wrapped around me like an old comfy shawl, bringing a smile to my face as I recalled the days of old. Passing the building where my family and I lived, I looked up at our fourth-floor apartment, trying to see if I could get a glimpse of the current residents and see the faces of the people occupying the room I once shared with my siblings.

I began imagining the lives of the children living in my old room; I wondered about the placement of their beds— are they facing the window so the sun is the first thing they see upon waking? Do they have posters (of Micheal Jackson and Cindy Lauper, if they have good taste!) plastered all over the walls, as I did? I thought about the god-awful floors and wondered if they still made that awful creaking sound with every step (even the lightest steps sounded like a Tyrannosaurus had entered the room). Did they paint over the heart I drew at the bottom of my side of the window, with the initials A.M & M.J forever, at the center?

Looking up at my old room, for a brief moment, time stood still. A figure of a girl appeared by the window where black and white striped curtains moved with the wind; I tried to see if the picture I painted in my head was anything close to how she kept the room, but I could only see figures coming in and out of the room. The window and building began to look like a scene from an old movie, where I was the main character trying to reenact old scenes from a time that no longer exists.

No matter how prepared or knowledgeable we are of the many milestones that are normal and expected parts of our development, that knowledge doesn't take away or lessen the nostalgia and fear one feels when faced with life-altering changes. While I knew I had no desire to live on this block or in that apartment again, I needed to be there. It was important for me to see and feel the energy of a familiar place.

Walking past beautiful tree-lined streets, with buildings offering a glimpse into the city's rich past, I could hear the sounds of children talking and running to the bus stop from my old elementary school. I thought about my schoolmates who, like me, have moved on, teachers retired, some buried. The corner store, known for its one-dollar hero sandwiches (turkey and cheese with light mayo), was now a pharmacy.

I remember feeling the need to stop, stand still, and take in the sights and sounds of my past, vaguely apparent in the present. I remember wishing I could walk through familiar streets again, wave and banter with familiar faces. I wish I could go down the boulevard and see the elders who once looked out for me, yelling at me to lower the volume of my walkman while crossing the street. I knew I had outgrown that time in my life and knew the person I am and desire to be would not fit in this current landscape, but when in the middle of a major change, where you're forced to enter new ground, returning or staying in the familiar, no matter how stagnant or toxic, is easier than the unknown.

Be still, not just in movement but also in thought.

There are three reasons why this season of stillness is challenging for most if not all, new empty nesters: Stillness forces us to be present, acknowledge our fears, and answer questions usually added last on our laundry list of must-dos. It forces us to examine who am I, if not a caretaker. We are forced to reconsider and possibly change how we see ourselves and the world around us. Questioning our need for approval and acceptance of how others will receive our desire for an improved self.

Learning to embrace your season of stillness and give your mind and body space and grace to make sense of the changes happening around you is the first step in creating a purposeful life after drop-off. Adapting to the stillness that comes with an empty nest can be challenging. As full-time parents, it's easy to push your feelings and needs aside, as the focus is on the family, with very little personal time to stop and focus on your individual needs and emotions.

In comes empty-nesting, a period where a big chunk of the time previously filled with activities and needs of your children is now left wide open with plenty of time to think and examine your values, aspirations, needs, and fears. It's quite an anxiety-filled concept. Especially for those who have mastered the art of being too busy to feel and explore their individual why. Exploring your identity beyond your role as a parent is one of those things that's often interpreted as not liking or enjoying your role as a parent. Parents, specifically mothers, are held to a standard where there is little to no room to voice the many challenges of parenting, specifically those associated with feelings of loss— loss of identity, time, and individual why.

Finding the courage to voice your love for your children and appreciation of all the beautiful milestones and experiences that come with motherhood while also sharing the many challenges and changes, both internally and externally, associated with parenting a child from the crib to the dorm room, is a significant part of embracing moments of stillness found in your empty nest years.

Parenting offers the noise many use to distract themselves from answering uncomfortable questions integral to our growth and reinvention of self. Stillness forces us to look inward and fully address those things that were swept under the rug during child-rearing, forcing us to see instances where we may have used parenting as a crutch to remain who we've always been and do things as they've always been done.

It brings to the forefront unhealed trauma that may delay our ability to reach our potential and asks us questions that enable us to reconcile the pain and regret of dreams deferred during child-rearing. Learning to embrace and appreciate your season of pause and marinate in your thoughts, exploring your biggest, most unimaginable options, and addressing feelings of purposelessness and fear of the unknown, is by far, the most challenging part of the beginning stages of life as an empty-nester— but it is so worth it.

It is in our moments of stillness that we have the opportunity to reacquaint ourselves with who we were before becoming parents, explore who we could be, and put to rest expectations that are not in alignment with the life we wish to live moving forward. No matter where you are in your empty nest journey, who you are, and who you choose to become in your empty nest years depends significantly on your ability to receive the messages conveyed to you in your moments of stillness.

Pushing through fear associated with moments of stillness requires an understanding that those uncomfortable feelings, emotions, and thoughts are not everlasting. While some feelings, thoughts, and emotions come to teach us a lesson, more often than not, most do not require fixing or redirecting but need space to run their course.

Allowing yourself the freedom to feel all feelings without shame or the need to fix them strengthens your ability to determine feelings that are factual versus those associated with unhealed trauma or unrealistic societal expectations. The road to embracing stillness is similar to the daily work needed to overcome fear. At the beginning of every major life change or act of faith is a heaviness or looming cloud of fear that can only be conquered by our ability to hear and recognize truths that can only be heard in our moments of stillness.

At any moment, we all have the choice to step back and let go of our perception of what stillness is and is not. Once we let go of our fear of being still, we discover the surprising truth of clarity. Most of us are, by nature, fixers; our brains are wired to problem-solve. In most situations, we are expected to think and move quickly; moving with urgency has become synonymous with moving with purpose. As women entering such a transformative season, it is important to understand the root cause of your fear of stillness and concur those fears before making permanent decisions.

For a long time, I struggled with the idea and practice of embracing stillness. When I considered the underlying beliefs that fed into my aversion to stillness, it became apparent that I, like many of you, operated from a place of scarcity. I grew up in an environment where not having enough (money, time, love, etc.) was part of the fabric that determined who I was and who I could be. For a long time, all of the myths associated with scarcity were a major part of my mindset and could be seen in how I approached my career, personal life, and self-care. Through the appreciation of stillness, I found the clarity needed to address and put to rest the scarcity mindset that shaped my who, why, and how.

When my youngest daughter entered her junior year of high school, I found myself in a state of panic. I became highly aware of my age and felt I was running out of time. I would cryptically say, "I'm closer to my sunset than my sunrise." I felt a clock was turned on, and I had a very short window in which to check off all the "must dos" on my bucket list and do those things I pushed aside to raise my girls; time was not on my side; I thought, so it's now or never.

Whether true or not, the idea that I was running out of time was all-consuming, clouding my ability to question and examine what was factual versus doom and gloom scenarios that, even to this day, have yet to happen. The belief that time was slipping through my fingers was crippling. I don't have much time left, I thought, and I could have managed it better in my youth. I knew those thoughts would be all-consuming if I slowed down and embraced moments of stillness. So, for a long time, instead of facing those thoughts and learning their root, I plunged into doing more and keeping busy for as long as I could.

But, like all things done at full capacity, you will reach a point where you are forced to find a healthy balance. Through embracing stillness and time alone, I learned that time was not my enemy and the only way to ensure I make good use of whatever time I have left is to be clear of my next steps and focus on those things that are in alignment with how I want to experience my second act. There is a rawness and splendor to life that can only be experienced when we resign to operate from a place of complete clarity and see things as they are and not as we imagined them to be, based on perceived lack or longing for what was.

It's been several years since my daughters graduated high school, and I can still remember how I felt when each of my girls left for University. While many things have changed for me and the girls, some of the greatest, most life-changing lessons I've learned about this journey were made possible through my willingness to embrace and nurture my moments of stillness.

When we live in the context of fully embracing and experiencing stillness, we learn to accept and navigate life as it is, distinguishing and taking full advantage of our resources and capabilities without the barrier of age, time, and defeating mindset. We engage in life from a place of abundance and understand that neither time nor age is our enemy. Our goal is not to simply check off every must-do and must-have off our bucket list but to create our own criteria for determining a well-lived life. I didn't come to this conclusion overnight, and as I write this book, I still have moments where old thoughts and habits stand in the shadows, waiting for the opportunity to creep in and consume me with doubt and yearning for a time long ago; you see, this kind of mindset change is like a muscle, you can't work on it every now and then, yet expect it to remain continuously strong; it's only as strong as the work you put into it.

Clarity through stillness

Clarity resides in us all. Cultivating an environment for it to appear and grow requires an intentional choice of how we think and appreciate times of stillness. Our relationship with stillness must move from, I must get through this, to I must go through this. Stillness is not something to push through and rush past to another task, person, or place. Instead, it is an experience that must be felt in a natural rhythm and pace to bring forth the power within us to see both internal and external resources available to us to create a meaningful life. Clarity brings truth; it separates facts from fiction and dispels myths. Operating from a place of clarity opens doors that will help you change your perception of self and the world around you. This will re-frame your understanding of stillness and position you to a place where you'll gain a new understanding and appreciation for what it is without fear of opportunities, experiences, and time passing you by.

I am not saying we have ample time and should operate from a place of having all the time in the world to reach our goals, nor am I disregarding the importance of being prepared. I understand fully that change, no matter how small, can prove difficult to accept and navigate. Since this particular season is filled with many unexpected bumps and turns, one would be wise to seek and create a preparedness plan. We would think it bizarre for a pregnant woman to reach her due date and not have prepared for the arrival of her newborn; why, then, would we not prepare for life after said child has left the nest? But preparedness without clarity is like washing your hands with the finest soap and drying it on the ground. Some of the greatest lessons I've learned about clarity have come from people who had expansive dreams but limited understanding of how to execute and bring those dreams to fruition and maintain them thereafter. To discount the importance of clarity in planning our second act, our approach to life after drop-off, and the opportunities afforded to us as empty nesters is to be a dreamer with no vision.

Each of us, through our willingness to embrace stillness, has within us all we need to create a meaningful and fulfilling life. But as long as we hold on to our fear of being still, we position ourselves to be in a place of constant doubt and belief that we are running out of time and resources. We must allow ourselves the freedom to fully embrace the gift of pause so we may gain a clear understanding of who we are and who we can become. Embracing stillness during major life changes fosters adaptability and mindfulness. It encourages us to acknowledge and not fear the uncertainties of transformation. Thereby enhancing our ability to successfully navigate the unfamiliar paths associated with life after drop-off.

Answer these questions in your next journal entry:

- In what ways have you learned to trust the process?

- Name someone who inspires you to live in the moment. What does that look like?

- What two habits have proven to be your reason for success?

- Name one thing you no longer have that you once thought you couldn't live without.

- It is the coldest Winter day of the year. Where are you? Name the first person you would reach out to in case of an emergency. Why them?

*"The power of finding beauty in the humblest things
makes home happy and life lovely."
–Louisa May Alcott*

This is Not Your Grandmother's Empty Nest Years

"There is not one big cosmic meaning for all; there is only the meaning we each give to our life, an individual meaning, an individual plot, like an individual novel, a book for each person."—**Anais Nin**

August 17, 2011 — Karma — Queens, New York

As I begin writing this chapter, I reach for my cellphone to put it on Do Not Disturb; one thing about aging and perimenopause that came as a complete surprise was how forgetful and easily distracted one becomes, and in my case, throw ADHD in the picture, and you have an energizer bunny with the attention span of a toddler. Setting timers for myself and using time management features readily available on my cell phone is the glue keeping me together, both socially and professionally. Right before putting my phone on Do Not Disturb, a message comes through from my friend, Sheila. Sheila is a single empty nester currently living in Aix-en-Provence, France, by way of Murietta, California.

We met in a Facebook group created for women over forty-five seeking information on the dos and don'ts of moving abroad. Her message reads, "You are so right we can't allow ourselves to approach midlife as our mothers did, neglecting to properly prepare for the inevitable hormonal, physical, and social changes awaiting us, and rely solely on our children to fill voids created by nature and poor planning, we must do better!" she wrote, ending her text with the hug emoji.

Our mothers are in their mid-seventies, and like most women of their generation, they spent most of their younger years working nonstop (if I'll sleep when I die was a generation, it would be Boomers) with little thought to what their sixties and beyond would look like. While they have mastered financial literacy and have meticulous plans for how they wish to be celebrated at death, most continue to remain clueless about what aging is and is not. Most failed to nurture a mindset in their fifties of, I'm getting older, which is a beautiful thing, but it's time I start paying close attention to my changing needs and physical abilities and not simply go with the flow, hoping my children will stand in-between gaps associated with those changes.

I know that in my own life, there are times when I feel like I have not done enough, not prepared enough, and found myself in situations where I just winged it. There are instances where going with the flow yielded great rewards and led me to experiences that were beyond my imagination and expectations. Looking back, I see two distinct reasons that often resulted in me having to or choosing to "wing it." One, occasions where I have done all that I can possibly do on my end, therefore, leaving it to God, the universe, or fate is the only option; or two, I am ill-prepared and stumbled into a situation that forced me to go with the flow.

When I first engaged the idea of what my empty nest years and approach to aging would look like, I knew that while some changes and experiences are inevitable and are expected parts of the aging process, my commitment to redefining aging would not yield meaningful results if I didn't make a conscious decision to focus on those things that are within my control. In doing so, I went back to basics, interviewing and seeking guidance from those who came before me. When you seek change and are willing to do what it takes to achieve said change, opportunities will present themselves in the most unexpected ways.

In late Summer 2011, it was discovered that I had a benign tumor in my uterus causing chronic anemia, leading to chronic fatigue syndrome. Due to the size and placement of the tumor, surgery was not immediate. I was instructed to take time off from work to rest while awaiting the opportunity for surgery. It was during that time, due to extreme boredom, that I decided to volunteer a couple of hours of my day at an assisted living community where I was part of the recreation staff.

While I don't have a musical bone in my body, I thoroughly enjoy acting and can do it relatively well. I, along with three other volunteers, was tasked with putting together an end-of-year play for the residents. What was supposed to be a six-week stunt turned into six months of learning and growth. I have, since the age of twelve, kept a diary or journal and made it a habit to journal daily, no matter the length of each entry or how eventless a day is. So, I was excited to document my time at the facility, as I knew the experience would be one of great value. To this day, reading entries from that time grounds me and provides the insight necessary for making choices that I hope will help future generations redefine aging and be active participants in their aging process. What began as a day filler and opportunity to entertain and bring a bit of joy to a population usually disregarded became the catalyst for me choosing to live a life of whys - why not me and why not now.

It was at the assisted living community that I met women, some older than my mother and some much younger, who gifted me the opportunity to see aging through their lived experiences. I remember one week in particular where I had the chance to sit with three of the more outspoken ladies at the facility, whose stories will forever be part of my why.

MARGOT

My first sit-down was with Margot, a 75-year-old widow born in Freeport, Bahamas, an island in the northwestern West Indies. Margot was petite but not frail; she wore a bright, vivacious, multi-colored shirt and pants set gifted to her by her son, Larry. Margot had a graceful and calm demeanor, a quiet strength in the way she carried the weight of her emotions. Her general countenance bore an unmistakable air of melancholy, etched deeply into the lines of her face. Her light cinnamon-colored eyes resembled sunset at dawn. Her gentle movements were measured as if every step she took was accompanied by the weight of memories that tugged at her spirit. She migrated to the United States in the sixties and had a long career as a flight attendant until retiring seven years ago, at sixty-eight years old.

Margot was very particular about where I sat in her room, not wanting me to sit on her bed with what she called "outside clothes." We sat on a large turquoise chaise situated at the foot of her bed, facing the garden. Her room was decorated with beach huts and nautical wallpaper in colors pink, turquoise, and yellow. A coastal wall art hung above her bed; island figurines and ornaments were meticulously arranged on her dresser, reflecting her island background.

Our conversation began with her sharing, in the softest, almost inaudible voice, that never in a million years did she think she would spend her last years at an assisted living community. She and her late husband were married for fifty-plus years, and while she had dreams of having a large family, she has one living son and three miscarriages. Positioning her son to have the life and responsibility that she, as an only child herself, had to deal with— being the only caretaker to aging parents until death. She knew all too well the difficulties of being the only child of aging parents and now, an aging parent with only one child.

"You say living in an assisted living facility was never part of your plan. Do you mind sharing your vision for this time in your life? What were some of your plans?"

"I didn't have a particular plan. I am West Indian; we don't abandon our parents or send them away. I thought my son would do for me what I did for my mother. I never told him as much, but he knew; it's how it is in our culture. Parents work hard and sacrifice time and sometimes health, knowing those sacrifices would be repaid by devoted children. That was the case for my cousins and many childhood friends, especially those with daughters. My plan, if you want to call it that, was praying that my son would marry someone who would show favor over me and encourage him to do for me what I did for my mother. I had hoped they would, by now, have a child or two, and I would be there to help raise them, but that has yet to happen. And at this point, I will probably be long gone when they decide to have a child." Margot paused, took a deep breath, sighed, and looked around her room, her gaze stopping at a frame that held a picture of her son with his wife. "I guess I should be content, and accept things as they are; he pays a good portion of my stay here, that's more than most parents can say or expect of their children, right?" She asked, still looking at the picture.

"Yes, that's very generous and kind of him; he sounds like a compassionate man. I'm curious, and you don't have to answer if you don't want to, but given the opportunity to plan a bit differently and knowing what you know now, what would you have done differently?"

Standing up, she walked across the room to a window where a small mid-century dresser stood; reaching for a round marble box, she opened it to reveal a vintage-style emerald-cut emerald gold ring.

"This belonged to my mother. It was one of her favorite pieces of jewelry, gifted to her by a gentleman friend when she lived in Panama. It has become my favorite and most cherished piece of jewelry in her collection. I reach for it when I miss her. You never forget or stop missing them, you know," she said, making small circles around the large emerald.

Her nails, painted with deep red nail polish, exuded an air of timeless sophistication and elegance. The glossy finish, when hit by sunlight, resembled rubies on her fingertips. The contrast made a stunning combination.

"Your parents, no matter how good or bad they may have been, or how long ago they've passed, there is always a part of you that forever yearns for their touch and reassurance that you're on the right path. I took care of both my parents right up to their last days. While I was, of course, employed during those years, they were my everything. My friend, confidant, and shoulder to lean on. I will forever cherish those years with them, but if I could do it all over again, I would make sure to create a community of my own. I would make it a priority to build a sisterhood of sorts. A sisterhood with women going through similar "changes" as I was at that time. Women who understood the challenges of caring for aging parents while going through the "changes." It's easy to lose yourself and neglect your own needs when caring for others. Given the chance, I would strive for balance. I would have focused on building a tribe."

Our conversation went on for about an hour. Margot shared bits of her childhood and expressed grief over her changing body and the woman she has become, so very different from what she had imagined. I listened attentively, acknowledging her grievances without showing pity or inserting my own fears. Aging is bittersweet; aging with regret for things that were within our reach yet we convinced ourselves were unattainable is devastating.

I still remember how I felt that evening, writing my first journal entry about our conversation; I remember feeling anxious as I could easily see myself aging with similar regret. While not an only child, I am the oldest and have always been a loner. I am independent to a fault, and if I am, to be frank, I feel much better alone than I do in a room full of people. I could stay indoors for days, with very little need for human interaction. Not being a people person or loner when you're younger is considered cool and admirable, but as we begin to age, being a loner is nothing to take pride in or see as a badge of honor. Having a community of like-minded women who understand and can relate to your current season in life is of the utmost importance in our fifties and beyond. That is not to say that one must have a large circle of friends just for the sake of being friendly, not at all. But a triangle of friends who get it, who get you, and who understand the importance of genuine, non-competitive, loving, and nurturing friendships is invaluable. Looking back at my journal entry of that day, I asked myself a question that I am asking you— you, who may share similar characteristics.

How will you build your tribe? What steps will you take to nurture existing friendships and create opportunities for true sisterhood without feeling suffocated?

ROSANA

My next sit-down was with Rosana. Rosana is eight years younger than Margot; she turned sixty-seven three days before our chat. Rosana was a first-generation Italian American, she was petite with a commanding voice and personality. Our chat started in the recreation room, where I found her going through what I later learned was her journal. We talked about my reason for volunteering and a bit about my children. Once she learned that I, like her, am a girl mom, she began to express the difficulties and differences she believe exist between raising girls versus boys. While never having or raising boys herself, she felt raising boys would have been more fitting of her personality. She was an educator by profession but could have easily taken comedy as a profession and thrived. Standing up from the lounge chair we were seated on, she pointed to a row of benches on the north side of the gardens, where she pretty much led the conversation.

"Do you believe in karma? she asked.

"No, I don't actually; why, do you? I replied.

We sat on a bench under a mix of evergreen and colorfully leafed deciduous trees overlooking a small pond. October in New York is magical. Making Fall one of my favorite seasons— changing leaves of red, yellow, and gold, makes for the perfect backdrop for this conversation.

"Of course I do; I'm Catholic. You reap what you sow is one of my favorite quotes, one I wouldn't mind if my children added to my headstone when I die. And I can see my oldest and middle daughters bullying my youngest daughter to go along with the idea," she said, half laughing at the idea. "If you ask my oldest daughter about my parenting style, she will say I am the ultimate unmotherly mother."

Shaking her left hand to adjust an assortment of vibrant and ornate bangles that exuded a sense of celebration and joy, a reflection of her vivacious spirit and carefree personality, she bent down to pick up a leaf and continued.

"I married and became a mother at a relatively young age. I was twenty when I had Lucia, my first daughter, with my second daughter, Francesca, coming four years later. We all pretty much grew up together. My first husband worked at a glass factory in Brooklyn. We were high school sweethearts. He died one year shy of his thirtieth birthday in a car accident; Francesca was just five years old. Anyone observing the dynamics of our household would say he was the nurturing parent in our relationship. Having grown up in a large family with two brothers and two sisters and being the beloved youngest child, he was undoubtedly our girl's favorite parent. Taking on the role of both mom and dad after his death stretched me in ways I never imagined. I could have easily moved in with my parents or his parents; they suggested as much, but I've seen firsthand how easily the child and parent dynamic can change for the worse when living and trying to raise your children under your parents' roof, so I didn't want to add another layer of confusion to my already challenging situation."

As I listened to her share her story, I began feeling uneasy and anxious even, I knew exactly where this was going and could already see why her daughter described her as unmotherly. I adjusted myself, pushed back my hair, relaxed my shoulders, and continued listening, making sure to be aware of my composure to ensure I didn't show any unfavorable emotions.

"You said your oldest daughter would call you unmotherly; how would you describe yourself in the context of motherhood?" I asked.

"Well, I wasn't a mushy or overly affectionate kind of mom, at least not with my oldest daughter. My situation required a strong and matter-of-fact approach, with my oldest daughter becoming my partner in crime. She filled the gaps previously filled by me when I had a husband. I was amazed at how quickly she rose to the occasion, taking on the role of helper, caring for her sister with very little fuss. It wasn't until I remarried and had my third daughter that I realized how much I depended on her and had groomed her to become a little woman. The teenage years were tough, and looking back, that was partly due to the fact that I never saw her as just a kid, you know what I mean?"

Before I could answer, "I connected with her as an adult for so long that I missed her entire childhood; heck, if you ask her, she would say she missed her entire childhood."

Her recollection of the parent she was to her oldest daughter sounds like something my own mother could share; there were so many similarities that, for a second, I felt I was talking to my mother.

"My relationship with my youngest daughter is different; my oldest daughter was already off to college when I had her, and my second was in high school. Parenting this time was different. My daughter was my husband's first child, and I was forty-one with much more clarity, cash flow, and support. My girls often tease me about writing a book about their childhood, with my oldest daughter joking that she would call it "The Many Faces of Mom." She doesn't recognize the parent I am with my youngest daughter, and for a long time, she couldn't wrap her mind around how different the two relationships are. If I let her tell it, she would say I play favorites, and she is my least favorite child, which couldn't be further from the truth. I love my daughters equally; they just met me at different stages of my life, which resulted in them experiencing versions of me created to deal with situations specific to a particular time in my life, you know what I mean?" she asked.

"Oh, I understand, I understand greatly. How would you describe your relationship with your daughters now?"

"You want to hear something unexpected? She asked, with a big smile on her face; she leaned closer to where I sat as if to whisper something she didn't want anyone else to hear. "Out of my three girls, my oldest is my biggest advocate, cheerleader, and confidant. God has truly blessed me through her. We have our issues, and I am still learning how best to approach her feelings of abandonment and loss of childhood. Through my relationship with my youngest daughter, I've learned that I didn't do enough and expected way too much of my oldest daughter; that is one of my biggest regrets in parenting. You have two daughters, right?" she asked.

"Yes, yes, I do."

"Life is unpredictable, and when it comes to your children, never put all your eggs in one basket. Love and provide for them equally, but always treat them based on their needs and personalities, not on who you need them to be to fit your expectations or needs. One day, they will be asked to tell their life stories, and you will be shocked to learn how different their recollection is from your own."

That Wednesday, when I left the assisted living community, I was both drained and incredibly uneasy. That conversation lasted no more than an hour, yet stayed with me the entire day and the rest of the week. When I returned to the facility on Friday, I knew exactly who I wanted to chat with. I was in need of hearing a different type of parenting style and thriving in your latter years, or at least a story that wasn't so close to home. While I have dealt with and have made peace with my issues with my own mother, part of the reason I have such a good relationship with my daughters is due to the fact that I surround myself with people whose life experiences and upbringing are opposite to what I saw at home. My motto is, "I know what didn't work in my relationship with my mother and what I didn't like growing up; position yourself to see and be around people who are living opposite to those pain points." On Thursday, the night before I was scheduled to volunteer at the facility, I placed a call to the coordinator asking to start a couple of hours before my usual schedule; I wanted to ensure I had the opportunity to chat with one of the facility's most exuberant personalities.

GENEVIEVE

As I walked past the welcome area, standing in front of the guest coatroom, I could hear the aromatic and rich, resonating sounds of a piano playing in the music room. It was early morning, with most residents still getting ready in their rooms or having breakfast in the dining room. Much like the recreation room and library, the music room is decorated on theme. European tilt-and-turn windows spun the entire width of the room, allowing plenty of natural sunlight to enter the room and an unobtrusive view of the gardens. The walls are tinted a soft, pale green, with sheet music covering the entire ceiling. The piano, placed near an off-white brick wall, is the perfect companion for the gorgeous, artistically engraved stone fireplace. I made my way to the music room, took a seat on one of the chaises just a couple of steps away from the fireplace, and listened as my third interviewee, seated at the piano wearing a flowy v-neck, silk tent dress with a mix of monochromatic floral prints, played the piano, Count Basie, April in Paris.

"I've always stood out. My father was German, and my mother was Afro-Argentinean and French. You wouldn't have known that if I hadn't told you, I'm sure. I inherited my paternal grandmother's porcelain skin and blue/green eyes, but my mother would say, 'Pay attention to the hair; the hair will reveal secrets that often get lost in light eyes,' said Evie (short for Genevieve).

With hair falling past her shoulders, she, at seventy-eight, has retained both length and thickness. Raising both hands to her head, she slid her fingers through thick curls that fell and covered both hands like white and silver cinnamon swirls.

"In my younger years, my choice of hairstyle was reflective of where I was in my life and who I was trying to be. I was born in Queens, New York, Astoria, to be exact. We lived in Astoria until my late teens, then relocated to New Orleans, Louisiana, where my father took a position as a university professor at Tulane University. It was there that my mother and I learned that I, like many in New Orleans, are what they called 'passe blanc,' people with African heritage who can easily pass as full White. Unlike in New York, where my mother allowed me the freedom of wearing my hair in its naturally curly state, in New Orleans, my choice of hairstyle and even clothes were strongly tied to creating an image that would not show any connection to my Afro-Argentinean roots. I lived in New Orleans until I married my first husband at the age of twenty-one. My husband, who was closer to my mother than I could ever be, was a carbon copy of my father. My mother was very pleased with his looks and background (German and Dutch); my marriage to him meant further dilution of our African ancestry. She was elated to have him as a son, while I simply wanted to get out of the house. You see, in those days, marriage was the easiest and most acceptable reason to leave home. I never had children, much to her chagrin. We did everything our finances and medicine could do, to no avail. Looking back, and I know this may sound crazy, but I think my inability to conceive was both physical and mental. As much as I loved my mother, a big part of me didn't want to give her the satisfaction of gloating about having a White grandchild. They say many of our physical ailments begin in our minds long before manifesting in the physical. I still believe I had a hand in not bearing children; not only was it, not a priority, but it was my way of taking control of my body and choosing to bring life to things that I find fulfilling and things that are not tied to who my mom or society said I should or shouldn't be."

I was intrigued by her demeanor and sense of clarity, which seemed to be gifted to her at birth. "Yes, I believe there is some truth to that. To some extent, what's believed in the mind has the power to grow and manifest in the body, both physical and mental. Have you any regrets?" I asked.

"About not having children? She asked before I could respond. "No, not at all. In my forties, friends would say, what about when you get old? Aren't you worried you will not have anyone to lean on or visit you when you're sick or too old to care for yourself? My response, then, remains the same today: having children doesn't guarantee companionship, loyalty, or personal health advocate. I am no more alone than any other woman my age. I have, in my eight years at this facility, seen women who sacrificed their health, youth, and time to raise children who remember them only when it's convenient. I have godchildren who check up on me regularly, and Just like I wasn't obligated to give my mother children to feed her insecurities and distorted mindset, children should not be seen as extensions of our retirement plans. I regret many things; not having children is not one of them. That's not to say I've had a perfect life; not at all. I've had my share of heartbreaks and made more mistakes than I care to share, but through it all, I pride myself in knowing that I did life exactly as I wanted and have the tattoo to prove it," she said, pointing to a small blue and red dragonfly tattoo on the inside of her right ankle. She explained that the dragonfly symbolizes carefree imagination, rebirth, joy, and transformation.

This chapter was one of the more challenging chapters to write as I saw myself and my upbringing in the lives of each of these women. As the oldest of four children, growing up during the height of the latchkey era, I have mastered the art of being alone without the need for a lot of human interaction. As an adult, I thrive best when I am alone. I enjoy social events, but my social battery runs out quickly. Cultivating a mindset where I don't operate like the lone woman on the island has been my greatest personal growth journey. Like Margot, my relationship with my mother, siblings, and children is my most important and cherished relationship. Learning the importance of having a tribe outside my immediate family and willingness to learn how to open myself to experience friendship without compromising my need for space and healthy boundaries is one of my most treasured gifts to my adult self, and the closure my younger self needed to move away from the mindset of doing life alone.

It is no secret that in most communities, families, friendships, and even in our marriages, the decision to seek another path and approach life differently than the expected norm, can lead to disagreements and disapproval of choices that may brighten the light on the insecurities of those closest to us. Desiring change or improvement of self can create an environment where we question our belief system and our need for a different life. The desire to do life your way, all while keeping the peace, going with the flow, and making the best of situations that may not fit our ideal life, can lead to feelings of regret and resentment. Who am I to want something different than what my family and peers think is enough for a person my age and background?

There are many ways to break free from living a life based solely on societal and familial rules and expectations. Choosing to take steps to improve yourself and how you show up in the world should not be tied to outrageous societal expectations of what's acceptable or unacceptable for a woman your age, race, socioeconomic class, dress size, or background. Rather, it is about how those improvements will position you to be the best version of yourself and create an environment where your life choices help to create the changes you wish to see in the world.

Consider this: we are all born with an internal fire, and much like an external fire, any flame requires three ingredients: oxygen, fuel, and heat. Lacking even one, a fire won't burn. Oxygen, being the easiest to have because of its relation to air, is the people you have in your circle. Since oxygen's role is to combine with fuel, fuel is your response and the relationship you have with those in your circle. Any number of sources may supply heat, your religious/spiritual beliefs, cultural/ethnic backgrounds and traditions, unhealed traumas, etc. Fuel is what burns, and almost anything can burn. Your ability or inability to control how you respond to the expectations imposed on you and engage in relationships that are in alignment with your ideal sense of self and community determines the temperature at which your fire will ignite and continue to burn.

Answer these questions in your next journal entry:

- How do you feel when put in a position where you have to come to a decision quickly?

- What amazes you most about your life so far?

- Finish this sentence: if my childhood best friend could see me now, they wouldn't believe that I am____.

- What one seemingly insignificant thing that instantly can change your entire mood from happy to meh?

- How do you stay connected with your adult children who may live far away or have busy lives of their own?

"To live is so startling it leaves little time for anything else." –Emily Dickinson

PART TWO
New Empty Nester

Whatever You Do — do not cry

"Almost every person, from childhood, has been touched by the untamed beauty of wildflowers."— Lady Bird Johnson

May 18, 2016 — It Is What It Is — San Diego, California

If you're reading this book, you might belong to one of two generations: Baby Boomers, born between 1946 and 1964 during the years following WWII, or Generation X, born between 1965 and 1980. While there are significant differences in how these two generations view the world, self, and parenting, both are experiencing changes that force the re-examination of old habits, belief systems, assumptions, and biases that shape their who and why.

With the youngest Baby Boomers being 58 years old at the time of writing this book and the youngest Gen X'ers at 42 years old, both have led lives where the definition of self is closely tied to financial success, external achievements, and their role as caretakers. Finding themselves at a crossroads where the reexamination of past choices and the desire to redefine self weigh heavily on their hearts and minds. They are pushed to ask questions previously avoided when raising their children and begin the journey of deepening their self-worth and self-perception outside of societal norms and expectations.

Today, we have at our fingertips access to all types of information, advice, and knowledge, but when it comes to the aging process, specifically, life changes occurring during our transition to life as an empty-nester and the many challenges of perimenopause and menopause, women often find themselves forced to suck it up and deal with the ups and downs of those changes, as quietly as possible. As a society, we often minimize changes that are deemed natural and normal parts of our development. The expectation is to experience those changes without fuss and make the best out of them because, well, it is what it is.

It was that way for our grandparents and parents, dealing with those changes without much ado; therefore, future generations should do the same. The expectation is to approach this season of our lives unquestioningly, speaking in passing, and experience it as we do an amuse-bouche—we may not like it, but we nibble, preparing the palate for what may or may not be a satisfying ending.

During my youngest daughter's senior year of high school, I found myself experiencing what I later learned to be perimenopause-induced depression. I remember a conversation with the mother of a close friend where I shared my apprehensions and fears regarding aging and menopause; while I am sure her response was rooted in the right place, her suggestion was to not make a fuss about the journey ahead of me, as millions of women who came before me had gone through these changes, some with very little resources or need for what she called, "babying."

While I felt disregarded and unheard, I knew her response was not rooted in a desire to be dismissive but closely related to her upbringing and the programming done to women to reinforce the idea that any show of emotions or concerning talk about the challenges of aging, body image and life as an empty nester translates to an inability to go with the flow and a reluctance to accept the inevitable and prepare to age gracefully.

Aging gracefully is a concept that has been woven into an experience that is far, far from graceful. Where those experiencing changes associated with aging (societal, physical, psychological, and contextual changes) are seldom offered the grace needed to shoulder those changes. That conversation and many others with women from all walks of life and backgrounds forced me to reflect on my own approach to life and aging, which meant understanding and defining the principles of my personal transformation. When I think about the process of transforming or reinventing oneself, I find myself remembering the parable or allegory of the pot roast. It goes something like this:

One day after school, a young girl noticed that her mom cut off the ends of a pot roast before putting it in the oven to cook dinner. She had seen her mom do this many times before but had never asked her why. So this time, she asked, and her mom replied, "I don't know why I cut the ends off, but it's what my mom always did. Why don't you ask your Grandma?" she suggested.

So the young girl called her grandmother on the phone and said, "Grandma, why do you cut the ends off the pot roast before cooking it?" Her grandmother replied, "I don't know. That's just the way my mom always cooked it. Why don't you ask her?"

Unremitting, the girl called her great-grandmother, who was living in a nursing home, and asked her the same question. "Why did you cut the ends off the pot roast before cooking it?

Her great-grandmother thought about it for a moment and said, "I cut off the ends of the pot roast because that's what my mother did. When I was first married, we had a very small oven, and the pot roast didn't fit in the oven, so my mother suggested I cut the ends off."

Truth or fable, this way of thinking and approach to life is not far-reaching. I am sure you can share stories of instances where your actions and thought process were not rooted in fact or even logic but on the basis of it's always been that way or done that way. If I look back at many pivotal moments in my life, I can see where discarding the possibility for change based on tradition alone resulted in many missed opportunities for improvement and growth. Where relying on tradition alone fostered a mindset of rigidity and inflexibility, which made it difficult to respond to unforeseen challenges and adapt to changing circumstances. We all have within us the ability to create the shift needed to thrive in this season of change. But we must first weigh those beliefs, traditions, and habits that have become part of our foundation and the measuring stick we use to determine how we present ourselves to the world, how we sit in our skin, and address challenges.

September of My Years

Imagine being part of a generation of trailblazers, women who, until the end of time, will be known as those who pushed the envelope and went against the status quo to determine their own fate and help pave the way for future generations. Baby Boomers, the first generation in history to fight and change the social landscape of the United States, grew up in an atmosphere of social change and radicalism. They reaped the benefits of an atmosphere of many freedoms. They are the first to view divorce as an acceptable option, and the first group of parents in the psychological era when seeking therapy became more commonplace, and relationships between parent and child were closely examined. They are the parents of the "latchkey kids," aka Generation X and older Millennials. They were passionate about teaching their children the importance of breaking glass ceilings and believing they could be whoever and whatever they wanted to be. They have now found themselves at a crossroads where they must learn to define who they are without their children.

For Boomers, who started midlife during a time when an empty nest meant an empty life, being intentional and focused on proper preparation for life after drop-off was an underdeveloped topic that remained hush-hush— recommendations on how best to deal with this season of life was done on an as-it-happens, fashion. Especially since many believe it to be a normal and expected part of parenting and aging, requiring little preparation or discourse. There wasn't a lot of precedent about how to do life after drop-off, and like many life changes faced by women in midlife, it was seen as something to go through quietly, with very little consideration for feelings of loss, and the anxiety one feels when going through such a process. While it is impossible to describe an entire generation accurately, there are widely regarded characteristics observed in each generation that point to the why and how of their parenting style, view of life, and what they believe their life should look like as empty-nesters.

For Baby Boomers, expectations regarding parental and child roles after drop-off may not be verbalized but are established long before the last year of high school. Statistically, they are known to value their family ties. Although the demise of the American family has been lamented throughout the boomers' lives, most continue to be actively involved with members of generations above and below them. They believe in caring for aging parents and see their children as their legacy. Born to parents who had to hustle really hard to provide for their family during a period of great economic instability, they spend more time with their young adult and adult children than their parents did with them and have a hard time letting go.

If we were to peel back years of characterizations and assumptions to take a fresh look at the why and how of baby boomers, we would begin to understand some very telling observations. Having been brought up by detached parents, many baby boomers find self-identity closely tied to their relationship with their children. Familial roles and expectations are well defined; for example, it's not uncommon for a baby boomer to plan their empty nest years around the belief that they will be expected to help care for their grandkids. Many look forward to it and verbalize their desire to be grandparents every chance they get. While not a bad way of looking at this stage of parenting, understanding that other options exist and choosing not to frame one's life around adult children and grandchildren is also an option worth exploring without shame.

Being a generation raised by parents whose idea of showing love and affection was closely tied to their ability to work hard and provide for the family, emotional support and providing space to explore all feelings and speak openly of those things that cause anxiety and distress was not a priority. Their upbringing was one in which their parents were hard workers, detached, and extremely committed to their work. This led to a laid-back approach to parenting, yet expecting their children to excel and approach life's challenges without fuss or need for much guidance.

Boomers, who were taught pretty early the art of keeping calm and carrying on, are finding it hard to openly share and express the roller coaster of emotions that comes with aging and life as seasoned empty nesters. Theirs was a household run by uninvolved parents that created a generation who took the opposite route and became helicopter parents to their Generation X and Millennial children. Micromanaging the heck out of their children, overwhelming them with well-curated activities and experiences. Parenthood is their entire life. They glamorize the idea of parenting by sacrifice, sacrificing their hobbies and social life for their kids.

As a generation with the highest divorce rate to date (between 1990 and 2012, the divorce rate for people fifty-five to sixty-four doubled. For those older than sixty-five, that number more than tripled), raising a latchkey kid (a child who is at home without adult supervision for some part of the day, especially after school until a parent returns from work) was not uncommon and required great sacrifices. And since their identity is tied to their willingness to sacrifice themselves for the betterment of their children, they fully expect their sacrifices to be repaid by children who will include them in all aspects of their adult lives and look to them to help navigate their lives and continue to be a major part of their empty nest years. Letting go and creating a life where their children are a significant part of their lives, but not the whole of it, is quite the challenge.

I remember a situation with a cousin who was in the process of purchasing her first home. She kept the entire process to herself, not sharing it with her parents or other elders in the family. She was proud that her hard work afforded her the opportunity to purchase her first house and wanted to surprise her parents after closing. Once invited to view the property after closing, her parents, although proud, did not take being excluded from the process very well. They felt such milestones and decisions should have been shared with them from the beginning so they could share input and be part of the experience.

This is not an unusual request; this thought process and need to be included is not uncommon for two reasons— family meetings started with Baby Boomers, bringing major life events to the table for all to dissect and provide input is a major part of their parenting style. parents who equate parental sacrifices to unconditional loyalty and access, any accomplishment experienced by their children is due to their sacrifices; therefore, deserve the opportunity to share input on major life events as that is part of the reward of parenting by sacrifice.

My mother, at the time of writing this book, is seventy-four years old, which puts her in the latter part of her generation. We have not always had a great relationship; raising four children as a single parent in Brooklyn, NY, is not for the faint of heart. If you had asked me ten years ago to describe my mother and our relationship, I would have leaned into the usual characteristics associated with her generation and would highlight most, if not all, of the negative characteristics associated with her generation— selfish, self-absorbed, demanding, overly-confident, yet highly co-dependent. If put on a strong face, even in the face of great sadness, uncertainty, and fear was a person, it would be my mother, and if it were a generation, it would be baby boomers.

It wasn't until I got married and had children that it hit me– she (during my entire childhood) was putting on a front. Masking her emotions, sidestepping talks about aging, and uncertainty regarding life as an empty nester are not simply examples of her being part of the most selfish and self-absorbed generation. But the residue of an upbringing where those feelings and life changes were not openly discussed. That realization felt like I caught her stealing from the cookie jar. Aha! I cracked the code. When asked to describe my mother, I not only refrain from using the usual descriptors that, more often than not, barely touch the surface of a woman with her past, but I make sure to remember that even the positive traits— resilience, self-reliant, ability to present a happy and hopeful disposition in-spite of current reality, are all trauma responses. Responses to trauma that, unlike other generations, are often overlooked when describing the who and why of Baby Boomers.

In our distinctly judgmental culture, which has now escalated into cancel culture, our attitude and relationship with generations who came before us is deeply rooted in a need to generalize, blame, and scrutinize, with very little room for learning the why behind individual habits and behavior. We demand accountability yet provide little to no room for rehabilitation and growth. While most Baby Boomers began young adulthood at an eight, on the opportunity scale, with them spearheading and benefiting from many firsts, their inability to openly express and discuss what they consider to be "private matters" with their peers and their children places them at level two on the emotional growth scale. Many lived a life of service to their country and close community, focusing on changing those things they believed to be unjust, outdated, and erroneous. Despite their achievements, they continue to struggle with bridging the gap between pioneer and relatability, hindering their transition from trailblazer to simply human.

While the identity of Baby Boomers is tied to sacrifice and family ties, Gen Xer's identity is tied to their ability to be of service to others, especially those who grew up with younger siblings. Being raised by parents whose parenting style is dubbed helicopter parents, parents who were never too far, yet too far to know and properly nurture their children's most basic wants and needs. Generation X's worth is closely tied to their ability to put the needs of others ahead of their own. Raised during a time when spending hours unsupervised after school was the norm, with many having to care for younger siblings, preparing their meals, and making sure to stay safe during those hours, Generation X's approach to life as empty-nesters mirror that of their upbringing, it's a one-person show.

They are the middle child, the forgotten generation— making them independent and self-reliant to a fault. While their parents shy away from seeking help or expressing those feelings that they deemed "private" out of shame, Generation X learned early to depend on themselves, with many choosing to navigate the ups and downs of life on their own, out of habit. They grew up when major changes, instabilities, and restructuring of family life and values were ongoing, where they didn't often have the brightest outlook on the future. This forced them to grow up faster than any other generation, perfecting the art of act first and cry later, which continues even in midlife.

While many boomers use guilt to ensure family connection and closeness continue after-drop-off, Gen Xers harbor guilt for possibly not doing enough or giving enough of their time and available resources. Even though their parents began parenting during the height of the use of outside help through therapy, it is Generation X who have utilized and benefited from the use of psychotherapy, making it part of their parenting and personal life to move past feelings of, should have, and could have.

Like all generations, their approach to parenting is greatly influenced by their desire to correct and do the opposite of their parents, seeking to correct what they deemed were missed opportunities in their childhood. As parents, they focused on giving their children those things not given to them in their childhood, which created a hyperparenting style. The thing about parenting from a place of giving your children those things you craved in your own childhood is that, more often than not, what ailed you as a child will not be the same for your children. It is never a good idea to nurture or pour into your children what your inner child still craves, as your children will, without a doubt, have their own needs that are opposite to what you desired as a child. Generation X's appreciation and willingness to include outside help in their who and why will undoubtedly help break generational barriers that could move them from the mindset of accepting life as the lone man on the island to embracing the power of authentic community and friendship.

Without judgment of good or bad, how true are those characteristics in your life? Whether you are a Baby Boomer or Generation X, entering this new chapter as an empty nester, deciding how you will present yourself to the world moving forward is closely tied to your ability to question outdated assumptions and give yourself permission to approach life with new sets of eyes. You have within you all you need to be a guiding light for your generation. Your willingness to question the unquestioned assumptions and myths about the empty nest years can lead to actions that help change the conversation and force the reevaluation of outdated and limiting cultural and societal expectations.

Answer these questions in your next journal entry:

- Think about the older women in your life; what do you admire most about their approach to life as empty nesters?

- Who is your biggest cheerleader, and what does that look like?

- What practices will you incorporate now that you hope to pass on to your adult children?

- What kind of fears motivate you to approach life with caution?

- It is Spring 2030— where are you, and what has been your greatest growth experience since becoming an empty nester?

"When we work with love, we renew the spirit; that renewal is an act of self-love, it nurtures our growth. It's not what you do but how you do it." — bell hooks

Pursue What is Meaningful — not what is accessible

"The reason people find it so hard to be happy is that they always see the past better than it was, the present worse than it is, and the future less resolved than it will be." — Marcel Pagnol

January 1, 2014 — Make it Rain — Brooklyn, New York

In my interactions with empty-nesters who have cracked the code for living life on purpose after drop-off, most, if not all, have three things in common: they are unafraid of living unconventional lives, are open to dreaming new dreams, and have trained their minds to recognize opportunities for new experiences, even when feeling compelled to call it quits. In early 2019, news outlets all over the United States were intrigued by seven Chinese girlfriends who pooled their money to buy and renovate a mansion in the suburbs of Guangzhou, a major city in southeastern China, to retire and enjoy their golden years together. They were colleagues who turned into best friends, with a friendship spanning two decades. The idea was said in jest in 2008; however, when one of the ladies found a 700-square-meter abandoned redbrick house, a silly joke became their reality in 2019.

Together, they built a modern three-story house with communal living space on the ground floor and private bedrooms for each of the ladies on the top floor. With an added tea room that boasts floor-to-ceiling windows overlooking expansive paddy fields. When asked why they chose such an unconventional living arrangement, they replied, "Ten or fifteen years from now, our children will be grown-ups, so we also hope that we can still be together in the next years. We joke that each of us should practice one skill so that we won't be lonely and fight with each other ten years later... Some can cook delicious food, some know many traditional Chinese medicine, some play instruments, and some grow vegetables," says one of the ladies. Such an idea is not the norm in China, a country where most empty nesters' dreams are closely tied to the generosity and obedience of their adult children. These ladies are, indeed, real-life 'Golden Girls.'

It is no secret that the world is aging rather rapidly; according to the World Health Organization, nearly two billion people worldwide are expected to be over 60 years old by 2050. People are living longer, and there seems to be a substantial social change happening globally; in countries like China, the population is rapidly aging; it was estimated that, by the end of 2020, Chinese empty-esters would have reached 118 million, accounting for about 50% of the total population.

While the tradition of multi-generational extended family living together continues to be very common, the percentage of empty-nesters living alone is on the rise. Such a phenomenon goes against the country's belief in Filial piety (*xiao*). Filial piety is obedience to role obligation where adult children are responsible for ensuring the continuance of their parents' happiness— not only by respecting their roles as elders but also by taking care of their financial needs.

Globally, life as an empty nester was never viewed in a positive light. Empty nesters were commonly depicted as sad, lonely, and depressed individuals whose dreams and plans were dependent on the willingness of their adult children to take on the role of provider, and nurture their parents' mental health, from midlife and beyond.

But similarly to the United States, where the American system places great responsibility on individuals to plan for their later years, and remain economically stable, Chinese society is slowly leaning toward a more individualist society. Where the focus on individual needs is increasing, the pursuit of privacy, independence, personal choice, and personal happiness is popularizing; and the importance of filial piety is slowly decreasing.

This type of change in social landscape is not only happening in China but also in countries like Japan, Italy, Germany, and Portugal. Home to the oldest citizenry in the world, dreams are being re-dreamed, and blank spaces are being added as placeholders to welcome new possibilities and experiences. Ushering in a new mindset where questioning cultural dreams and expectations is not seen as disrespectful or disobedient but an opportunity to explore options that can lead to a more intentional life. When we approach life with the mindset of pursuing what is meaningful and not simply go with what's available, we stand better prepared to shift and pivot when life-altering social changes occur.

In high school, I had a very close friend who, like me, was the oldest daughter in a single-parent household. Maxine had four siblings under her, and like many oldest children in single-parent homes, she had many responsibilities. We shared many similarities, including an obsession for all things old Hollywood glitz and glamour; we were thick as thieves. She taught me how to sew, a skill she learned from her maternal grandmother, who was a seamstress by trade. Sewing came naturally to Maxine, so much so that she would add patches to ripped jeans and jackets, repurposed old and torn clothes, and create new pieces with just about anything. What began as a hobby became a great help for a family of seven, helping to save money on the cost and maintenance of everyday clothes. By the time we graduated High School, she had transformed hundreds of pieces of old clothing, from oversized shirts to torn jeans and dresses, turning them into stylish outfits that would otherwise be outside her family's budget.

Seeing the financial impact of something that came so naturally to her sparked a desire to perfect her craft and birth a dream of designing a clothing line with proceeds going to children in need. Maxine went on to attend (FIT) Fashion Institute Technology in New York City, and in her twenties, worked as a fashion designer for many well-known brands. In her forties, after twenty-plus years in the fashion industry, she began the journey of redefining her why. Which meant listening to her soul and giving herself the freedom to truly explore reasons behind her chosen path, and determine her next steps. At forty-eight, while fashion design remains a significant part of her life, when I asked her to share why she didn't continue with her initial dream of fashion design, her response is one I often consider when determining my individual why.

"Some dreams are born out of necessity and need for survival. Creating beautiful pieces with just about anything will forever be part of my creative process, but I learned early (thankfully) that my dream of becoming a fashion designer did not come from a place of authentic passion but a need to remedy a void that as I got older and began healing, no longer needed filling. That's not to say I no longer have the desire to give back and share my success and gifts with others, not at all. I simply reached a point where, like old dreams, I no longer approach life, pursue experiences, and give back from a place of pain, but as a celebration of my peace," she shared.

Much like purpose, dreams are not finite; they change, and that's okay. One question frequently asked of teens that I wish would go by the wayside is, what do you want to be when you grow up? A question that is both limiting and, for those with no idea of their individual who and why, formulating a response so as not to look ill-prepared and clueless, can cause great anxiety, evoking feelings of shame and self-doubt. Such a question seems so finite. It's as if once you've picked a career or have an idea of what you'd like your life to look like, that's it! You enter the point of no return— such a limiting way to view one's future. Many of us, unfortunately, carry that belief well into adulthood. Where the thought or mention of exploring new opportunities, and experiencing life opposite of our original plan feels like a failure– a stain on our resume of life. Leaving little room for exploring new dreams or flexibility for tweaking our original plans.

I am not suggesting one should navigate life with little direction or plan; what I suggest is remembering that the future you dreamed for yourself in the early years of your youth may not fit the reality you wish to live in midlife. We all have the power to be a positive part of the shifts happening around us. As our world changes and our role in the lives of our children change, we must embrace the idea that multiple things can be true at once. When we approach change from a place of opportunity, we awake within us gifts that lie dormant, awaiting our attention to connect the dots and thrive in any environment.

When we give ourselves the freedom to examine the root of our dreams at every stage of our life, we position ourselves to fully appreciate dreams that are attached to our desire to remedy pain from our past, therefore, here for a season; versus those that can stand the test of personal growth and freedom of choice. I have, for the last seven years, done away with creating a list of New Year resolutions. I instead view my birthday as the beginning of my new year. It is then that I take a look at my choices from the previous year, evaluating my feelings and thoughts regarding my career, where and how I live, and how I present myself to the world; asking myself these three questions:

- Given the chance of a clean slate, with no judgment or fear of failing, would your choices be the same?
- If money, status, cultural and societal expectations were not part of the equation, would you still choose this life?
- Would your healed self choose this path?

Ask any woman in midlife, and they will tell you, one of the most asked questions of women in midlife is, do you miss your twenties or wish you could go back to those years? A rather odd question considering our twenties, for the most part, are the most people-pleasing years of our lives. Where most of our decisions, wants, and needs are closely associated with societal expectations and a desire to fit in– it is our copycat era.

While many would describe their twenties as their carefree era, where the willingness and freedom to try anything at least once is at the center of their identity, you will find, more often than not, their approach is what I call selective freedom. Selective freedom is where we give ourselves permission to experience and engage in those things that are safe and acceptable by society's standards and will not have us looking like the odd person out. We allow ourselves the freedom to be…just like everyone else. It is in our forties that we begin to question our choices from a deeper level and explore the possibility of a new representation of self, and embrace the idea that while we have one life, we can live many dreams. And if we're lucky, our fifties and beyond will be the Sunday of our twenties, without the need for societal validation or approval.

As you navigate life as a new empty-nester, feelings of fear, doubt, and desire to re-invent yourself will come and go. The idea of dreaming new dreams will be both fascinating and frightening. You will have moments where, no matter how dreadful the good old days were, you still wish time didn't move so quickly and that the life you built with your children could continue to satisfy your needs in midlife. Familiarity and contentment are identical twins; if you don't pay close attention to how each presents itself in your life, you will find yourself staying in places and in seasons that should be part of your past.

"Money is only a tool, it will take you wherever you wish, but it will not replace you as the driver." — Ayn Rand

No talk of dreaming new dreams would be complete without acknowledging the elephant in the room, the one barrier that plays a significant role in the reason many are apprehensive about dreaming new dreams or bringing old dreams to fruition. To tell someone to dream new dreams and pursue those things that speaks to their soul without considering their relationship with and access to money is irresponsible and tone-deaf. Especially since we as a society associate success and a well-lived life with how much or how little money one has. We uplift and devalue ourselves and others based on buying power, and access to material goods. Our relationship with money, depending on where we fall on the scale, manifests in two ways: it can be one of great privilege and power, with a distorted view of what joy and contentment is and is not, or one where our potential is stunted, self-worth discounted, where we approach life from a place of scarcity and lack. For most of us, our approach to life and measuring stick used to determine our who and why is closely tied to our ability to raise our net worth, which by society's standards will determine our self-worth. You have a lot = you are a lot; you have little = you are little.

I met Linda at a financial literacy workshop at Hunter College in New York, NY. The six-week seminar was created to guide participants through the home buying process, from learning the ins and outs of individual credit scores to tips on how to successfully apply for loans available to first-time home buyers.

"I've never had a good relationship with money; as someone who grew up in a resource-poor environment, I learned early that money is hard to come by and rarely stays when it comes. Growing up, we never had large sums of money just sitting in a bank, but we had what we needed to survive. So, when I got older, I chose a practical career, one that offered job security and good pay. You don't have the luxury of doing what you love when in an environment where no one is coming to save you, and opportunities outside of those associated with STEM (Science, Technology, Engineering, and Mathematics) degrees are far and few. My biggest fear was not having enough. The first ten years of my career were all about the hustle, but like most people raised in resource-poor environments, money left as fast as it came. I lived a life of luxury long before learning how to sustain it. If putting the horse before the cart was a thing, it would be my relationship with money. I wanted everything that symbolized that I had made it and, therefore, worthy of existing in my skin. In the past year, I've had more losses than wins, not because of lack of opportunity or access to have or make more money, but a gross misunderstanding of how to use it."

I read somewhere that if you want to know where your priorities lie, check where your money goes and grows. It doesn't take a fortune to live an abundant life, but we must first understand what money is, its role in our lives, and how to use it to represent our core values. In my own life, money was a means to an end. I grew up in a very religious home where the attitude towards money was, at times, extremely confusing. Money is the root of all evil, was my introduction to what money is and isn't. Money is to be used, not saved, because God will provide (even when we misuse and spend it irresponsibly).

My introduction to money framed what I believed was the role money should play in my life. Being able to buy more stuff and willingness to work hard to make more money, shaped my understanding of my role in how money entered and left my hands. My understanding of money was that it was hard to come by and is evil, yet it is the measuring stick that I should use and society will use to determine my worth. I had, for a very long time, an extremely toxic relationship with money; I hated how it made me feel when I had it, and I hated it even more when it seemed to elude me.

When I decided to repair my relationship with money, I approached it like a child who had no knowledge of its power, with no pre-existing money traumas or expectations of what it can and can't do. I went back to basics, removing all emotional ties, relearning what money is and isn't, how and if God played a role in my having access to it, and how best to use it and still remain true to my core values.

Money is an invention with no intrinsic value. It is an object with a value placed on it, allowing for the trade of goods and services. Since its invention some 5,000 years ago, from the shekel, created by Mesopotamian people, to modern-day e-payment systems, money has been at the center of some of the most impactful changes in human history, leading to some of the most significant and most vital moments for many nations.

At the most toxic point of my relationship with money, I allowed my misunderstanding of its role in my life to dictate the trajectory of my career, avoiding proper salary negotiation all for the sake of not wanting to appear greedy or driven by its evilness. After years of hearing my peers complain about being overworked and underpaid, I convinced myself that not having enough was part of the human experience in the workplace. I adopted an "it is what it is" mentality to avoid conflict and pacify my disappointment.

One of the biggest myths and barriers to having a good relationship with money is the idea that we should accept how it enters and leaves our hands, without questioning our role in the handling of it, and the role of those who take advantage of people who lack a proper understanding of its flow. When we adopt an "it is what it is" mentality, we accept that there is partiality in who gets to have and keep money, who gets to have and maintain peace, and who gets to have and experience joy. We convince ourselves that some things just don't happen to, or for people like us; leading to a victim mentality that stifles our creativity and productive abilities. For those with deep-rooted religious beliefs, God is blamed for not giving enough, or not putting them in positions to make more; forgetting that God, was never in the making and distribution of money, to begin with. And, even if he were to give them access to more, their misunderstanding of the flow of money would lead back to a negative balance.

Money by itself isn't the problem. Wanting more money isn't evil. The desire for more of anything is innate and nothing to be ashamed of. Ask anyone who's ever had a relationship where they loved and lost someone what they wish for most; many will say they wish they had more time. Ask solo travelers returning home from their first trip to describe one highlight of the trip, and they would share an appreciation for the peace that comes with traveling solo, and wish for more peace in their everyday lives.

Wanting more money is neither greedy nor evil. When you address your desire for more money head on and gain a proper understanding of how it can and should flow in your life, you realize that what you desire is not to hoard large sums of money for the sake of having money, but to direct whatever amount you have, in ways that enables you to have a meaningful and joy-filled life. Having a clear understanding of the role of money, understanding your role in how it enters and leave your life, is of the utmost importance when exploring the possibility of dreaming new dreams, and embracing your why not me, era. Having a balanced approach to money, where it serves as a means to support one's aspirations and well-being, rather than being the sole determinant of happiness, and understanding that money is a tool rather than the ultimate source of contentment, will allow you to discover abundance in simplicity. Where living a joyful life isn't contingent upon amassing vast riches; but more so living a life where you fervently embrace gratitude, meaningful relationships, and experiences that enrich the soul.

Embrace your aspirations fervently, pursue your dreams with unrelenting determination, and let your passion drive you forward. But do so with clarity of thought, and understanding that, while you may not have the power to control all aspects of this journey, if you remain flexible and adaptable to change, embracing all opportunity for growth and new experiences, you open yourself to experiences that are beyond your wildest dream. Life as we know it, is wildly unpredictable, circumstances might shift unexpectedly. But don't mistake having to take another route, or exploring other methods for realizing your dreams as failure, or an indicator that you're on the wrong path. Being open to change or taking another route doesn't imply giving up on your dreams. It involves a willingness to adjust your methods without losing sight of the ultimate goal. If you were to curate a list of words to live by during this stage, I would suggest adding, flexibility. Flexibility allows for innovation, resilience, and the capacity to seize unforeseen opportunities that could lead to even greater fulfillment in pursuing your dreams. It fosters a midset where those open to it, embrace the balance between unwavering determination and the adaptability needed to navigate the twists and turns of this journey without losing sight of their overall who and why.

Have you ever witnessed someone performing a craft, or living what many would deem a simple life and think, this person was made for this. When you ask someone to share a dream they would like to bring to fruition, or a way of life that speaks to their soul, they immediately think it must be something grand or unimaginable. Your dreams and lifestyle don't have to be larger than life, or revolutionary to be deemed worthy of pursuing. They can be as simple as creating an atmosphere at home that resembles the peace you feel when laying on a remote beach. The excitement you feel when carving out time to learn a musical instrument or multiple languages. Your dreams do not have to be elaborate to be worth dreaming or exploring. But you must not let your dreams, cloud your vision. Weighing your dreams to determine what they represent and what they come to feed in you, is of the utmost importance. Some dreams are part of our story since birth, while others are added by us to feed a need, or pacify unhealed wounds. They become roadblocks, delaying us from getting to where we are supposed to be. Never stop dreaming, but do so with both eyes open.

Answer these questions in your next journal entry:

- How do you respond to the phrase "it is what it is"?

- What does abundance look like in your life?

- What pressures in your community regarding aging would you like to see go by the wayside?

- When do you feel most at peace?

- You have the opportunity to speak with any woman in history or from your past; what are you two talking about?

"The most essential factor is persistence—the determination never to allow your energy or enthusiasm to be dampened by the discouragement that must inevitably come."
- Mary Kay Ash

Get Off The Pedestal

" In the midst of winter, I found that there was winter me an invincible summer. And that makes me happy. For it says no matter how hard the world pushes against me, there is something stronger— something better pushing right back." — Albert Camus

March 28, 1986 — Who Do You Say I am? — Brooklyn, NY

It was the last week of March and the last day of the marking period. As I sat on a bench in my junior high school gymnasium, watching my peers prepare to complete the last obstacle course of the semester, I'll never understand why rope climbing is a mandatory skill for 12-year-old children. What situation will I find myself in where rope climbing is the one skill that can save me or is the determining factor of my success? I thought. I'm not prepared for this. Rarely am I emotionally or socially prepared for gym class.

At the beginning of the semester, I wrote a letter to my guidance counselor, asking to be excused from gym class on the grounds that the mandatory gym uniform (gold shorts and blue T-shirt) goes against my religious beliefs. Two days before the beginning of gym class, I overheard a conversation between two religious girls, with one saying she and other religious girls were excused from wearing the mandatory uniform due to religious reasons. Naturally, I thought I'd try my luck and claim the same. While I'm not part of their religious sector, pants and shorts are, in fact, unacceptable clothing options for girls and women in my strict Pentecostal church, so I was not wrong in seeking the same consideration.

Physical Education (PE) was my most hated subject and a complete waste of time. Having to perform and be tested on physical abilities while your peers watch as you sweat, hyperventilate, and trip over scrawny chicken legs and duck-like feet is far from character or strength-building. Physical Education (PE) was the last class on my schedule. Since most students preferred to have gym class as their last class of the day (to avoid going through the day smelling like sweat and shame), that time slot had the largest student-to-teacher ratio, making it the most crowded gym class of the semester.

We were divided into groups of six, with the first letter of our last name determining who within the group would go first, second, and so on; it was one of those moments where I wished my last name was Williams or Zenith. Whether first or last name, I always found myself going first or second. With eight teams consisting of six students in each team, standing in alphabetical order in front of two lines of large tires, three extra-large hula hoops, a blowup slide, monkey bars, and a rope climbing wall, I was set to go second. Anyone peeking through the semi-glass doors would be shocked to see that a good portion of students, usually talking and carrying on way too loud in the hallways, are in here barely breathing, nonetheless talking. The silence is palpable, with each student lost in their own thoughts and anxieties, awaiting the signal from our gym teacher to begin the obstacle of shame. Like clockwork, I began to feel tightness and pain in my right palm. A sign that has long been my body's way of alerting me that bad news or a bad outcome is near.

Rubbing the inside of my hand with sweaty fingers that felt like mush, I adjusted my shorts, desperately wishing the bell would ring or a tornado would swirl through the gymnasium and swallow us up; my anxiety was at an all-time high, "I hate this," I whispered. And then it happened, while not quite a tornado, the double doors of the gymnasium swung open, and in came an office monitor waving a hall pass side to side, running past lines of anxious students to reach our gym teacher, Mr. Ross. We all knew what her presence meant; someone was about to be taken to the Assistant Principal's office. As much as I wanted to be excused from gym class, I knew being asked to go to the office was just as bad, if not worse, than having to take part in the obstacle of shame. All eyes went to Mr. Ross, who was looking down at the hall pass handed to him by the office monitor; he looked up, stared right at me, pointed to where I was standing, and, with his right index finger, signaled me to walk over to where he and the office monitor stood.

What should have been another cold and gloomy Winter day in Brooklyn was surprisingly one of the month's warmest and most beautiful spring-like day. Seated in the backseat of my neighbor's orange Volkswagen Beetle, the compact interior and curved roof felt suffocating, and I don't remember the engine being so loud. I rolled down the window, hoping the feel of fresh air would help calm my anxieties. I secretly wished it was a cold, dark, cloudy day, as judging by my neighbor's tone and body language, there was nothing beautiful about this day. "Your mother is not home; she fainted shortly after you left for school and was taken to the hospital. You will have to stay home from school to look after your brother and sister until we know more, and I will check on you guys before I leave for work and at bedtime," she said.

I remained quiet, incapable of formulating a response. For as long as I can remember, whenever I am faced with uncomfortable, painful, or sad situations, my voice is the first to go. "Are you listening? Did you hear what I said?" she asked. Still looking out the window, I nodded up and down in what was supposed to be yes, "yes, I heard you," I whispered. I heard her but didn't understand. What did she mean mommy fainted? She was fine when I left this morning. What about the baby? Is she okay? I thought.

Passing our neighborhood park, which sits one block away from our apartment building, we stopped at a red light, and I could hear and see children playing on the monkey bars while others skipped rope, shouting, "Nickel and dime be on time when the school bell rings at a quarter to nine..." that image felt like I was looking at my past, and as we began driving off, the less I was able to hear the sounds of the children singing, the more it felt like my childhood, my innocence and life as I knew it, is no more.

I didn't know the severity of my mother's condition. I knew she was pregnant, but if there were issues with her pregnancy, I would be the last to know. I am part of a generation of kids raised by men and women who believe children should be seen and not heard. Adults in my world didn't share much with their children, especially in situations that presented them as weak, sick, or incapable of governing their bodies and everyday life situations. For the first time in my life, I would much rather be back at gym class than prepare myself for what I feel awaits me in the coming days and months.

After what felt like the longest three days alone in our three-bedroom apartment, with my neighbor checking in on us each morning before leaving for work and evening before bed, I was finally taken to the hospital to see my mother, "If they ask you your age, just say you're thirteen," my neighbor instructed. I nodded, whispered an unconvincing yes, and began massaging my right palm. Walking towards the information desk, I felt like I was being dragged through the corridors while carrying a ton of bricks. My neighbor did all the talking, telling the receptionist that I am thirteen and have visited my mother before, so there shouldn't be a problem with me visiting her now. We were handed two guest passes and directed to take the visitor's elevator to the maternal intensive care unit (MICU) on the ninth floor.

Nothing says life and death like the sounds of machines connected to a lifeless or sickly body. This was my first time walking through an intensive care unit; I had no idea what to expect. My expectations were solely based on images seen on my favorite television shows. But even they didn't prepare me for the coldness and matter-of-fact feel of the ninth floor. As a latchkey kid, my days after school were spent watching ABC after-school specials, but on days when I stayed at my neighbor's house, I was glued to the television watching Daytime Soap Operas. Most days, I could make it home on time to watch General Hospital. This played a role in my envisioning a scenario where my mom is lying lifeless on a cold bed with doctors, nurses, and staff crowding around her, doing whatever it took to keep her alive.

While the crowd was smaller than I imagined, cold and direct were spot on. The image of my mother on a hospital bed surrounded by machines and well-placed cords attached to her temperamental body while extending her hand to get a feel of the person entering her hospital room will stay with me until my last breath. "Who's there? Who's that?' she asked. Turning her head in my direction and lifting her right hand to touch and feel the person approaching her bedside, my strong and resilient mother, with eyes that can simultaneously evoke feelings of fear and comfort, was blind.

My mother was six months pregnant with my youngest sister when she developed pre-eclampsia, causing temporary blindness in both eyes. Unable to make sense of the image before me, I walked quickly toward her bedside, adjusting the ill-fitted yellow hospital gown given to me by the nurse. I could feel tears beginning to fill my eyes; I reached for her hands and leaned in as close as the cords, machine, and clunky hospital bed allowed, "It's me, Mommy, can you see me? Can you see me, Mommy? It's me. I'm here now, Mommy," I said, holding her hands while ensuring I don't move or disrupt the cords attached to her hand and chest.

My mother was hospitalized for three of the longest months of my childhood life. Looking back, I don't know how I survived and successfully passed seventh grade. Her recovery was slow, and according to doctors, it is a miracle that she lived to share her story. While I've always associated my mother's ability to navigate life unafraid, resilient, yet graceful, to an unwavering zest for life and superhero-like characteristics, this situation elevated her to god status. My twelve-year-old self made a god out of my mother, putting her on a pedestal that, for a long time, made it difficult to see the human side of her. From the day she was discharged from that hospital in 1986 to my late thirties, my mother could do no wrong, or I, at least, refused to acknowledge her flaws and shortcomings. I put her on a pedestal where she had very little room to be human, making it impossible for me to engage, rationalize, and love her as the flawed individual she is.

For children who grew up in what many would call intense home environments, witnessing trauma that forces them to grow up faster than most, and placed in situations where they had to be "little women"(expected to respect and honor their parents and elders as children should, all while performing and rationalizing life's ups and downs as adults), aggrandizing their parents, turning them into gods and goddesses, is inevitable. Which in return puts them in positions where they are perpetual servants. It wasn't until my late thirties, through much healing and therapy, that I was able to take my mother off that pedestal. Allowing me the clarity to see the human and woman sides of her. Which gave her the space and freedom to engage me with vulnerability and love that goes beyond the child and god-like relationship created by me in my youth.

To say I had an extremely unhealthy attachment to my mother is an understatement—a fact solidified by an encounter I had during a church service back in 1988. One evening during a weekly church service, a woman who was well regarded by the congregation walked up to me and my mom and "prophesied" that due to my placement as the oldest child and having experienced firsthand the many ups and downs of my mother's parenting journey, I will forever be my mother's side-kick. Bending down to where I was seated, looking into my eyes as if to make sure her next sentence permeated through every cell in my body, "I hope you understand how lucky you are to have your mother here with you today. Her ability to pull through after what she's been through, is nothing short of a miracle, never forget that," she said. No pressure, right?

I believe that I and numerous other firstborn children who grew up alongside young parents, seeing firsthand the rollercoaster and challenges associated with inexperienced parenting, develop an emotional imbalance where we operate and engage with our parents from a place of extreme emotional empathy.

Emotional empathy is about sharing feelings with others to the extent that you may experience pain when watching someone in pain or experience distress when watching someone in distress. It is said to be the first type of empathy that any of us feel as children— often seen when babies react to a smile or the sound of another baby crying. Emotional empathy can be both good and bad. It plays a vital role in our ability to appropriately respond to family and friends when they are distressed, and as in my case, can be used as a crutch, clouding my ability to objectively analyze people and situations for who and what they are; which inevitably lead to empathy overload.

If you're reading this book from the seat of a mother whose children have elevated to god-like status, I can't stress enough the importance of getting off that pedestal. It's easy to get comfortable on the pedestal that is flawless, unquestioning motherhood. If you search for the meaning of mother in any dictionary, you will find that its meaning is virtually endless, and many of the adjectives used to describe motherhood are closely similar to those used when describing God or a god-like figure (i.e., selfless, unafraid, strong, unwavering...), leaving very little room for those very human characteristics and experiences that shape our why and who.

As you navigate this new season, allow yourself the freedom to show up not only as a mother, wife/significant other, but give yourself permission to show up as the ever-evolving, flawed, and multi-faceted human that you are. A woman who is fully aware and accepting of her flaws, unashamed to show vulnerability, and open to redefining her who and why without the weight of living and portraying a perfect, strong, all-knowing being. Motherhood doesn't end after drop-off. Nothing is more beautiful and fulfilling than nurturing and growing a healthy relationship with your adult children. That, too, is a vital part of living an intentional and fulfilling life after drop-off.

Many of the challenges you will face during this new season are closely related to how well you're able to accept the inevitable role change that happens in this phase of parenting. Your understanding of the steps needed to navigate this season successfully lies in your willingness to embrace, relearn, and proactively seek help when those changes and expectations are outside your comfort zone.

Being able to relate with your adult children from a human perspective, devoid of judgment and need to be seen as an all-knowing deity, will position you in a place where you engage with them from a place of empathy and healthy friendship. You must now be to your adult children, the grandparent you would be to your grandchildren (that is not an invitation to pressure your children into having children!). Vulnerability, acceptance, and willingness to look in the mirror when dealing with the rollercoaster of emotions that comes with this season, all while empathizing and gently guiding your child while they begin to make sense of their who and why, is of the utmost importance when bonding and creating an intentional relationship with your adult child.

If you allow it, the growth experienced during your years as an empty-nester can strengthen existing bonds and be a critical factor in rebuilding upside-down relationships with your adult children. Your willingness to remove the mask and allow your children to see the human side of mom will lead them to fully appreciate the woman you are and the woman you wish to become. As you continue to make sense of your next chapter, you will have moments where you will question past decisions, and depending on where you are in your growth process, you will lament over those things that should have and could have been, wishing you were given at childbirth, a booklet of do's and don'ts of parenting children from crib to drop-off.

One of the greatest lessons and my secret sauce for finding joy in this season is inviting my daughters to walk beside me on this journey. Sharing my ups and downs and engaging them as young adults who are both wise and reflective has helped me better identify and appreciate growth opportunities and make peace with my long list of could haves and should haves.

As I write this chapter, my mother, at seventy-four, continues to be the one person who comes to mind when I am asked, who do you turn to when faced with a challenge, or as the young people say, when "life is life-ing"? While I no longer look to her or expect her to be my superhero, her willingness to relearn and embrace new ways of parenting adult children, plays a significant role in my approach to thriving in my empty nest years.

Answer these questions in your next journal entry:

- How will you finish this sentence: Dear younger me, you will never believe_____.

- Who do you turn to when life is challenging?

- What's your comfort movie?

- What role did religion play in developing your parenting style?

- How do you maintain a sense of fun and playfulness in your relationship, even as you face the responsibilities of midlife?

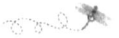

PART THREE
Seasoned Empty Nester

Chasing Happy - Choosing A Lifestyle

"Love is that condition in which the happiness of another person is essential to your own." — Robert A. Heinlein

February 11, 2017 — Write Your Story — Los Angeles, California

We met online in a Facebook group created for women over forty-five looking for tips and tricks for solo traveling. We were both empty-nesters; while I was new to this type of parenting, Evelyn was a seasoned empty-nester. We chatted on and off in the group and soon began chatting privately via Instant Messenger. Where we learned quickly that we had much more in common than we had differences. Her children, ages thirty-four, thirty-two, and twenty-seven, have long left the nest. Her oldest daughter lives overseas in Japan, while her two youngest children live on the East Coast. She and her husband of thirty-seven years live in California, in the same house where they raised their children. We talked about the joys of motherhood, the ups and downs of peri-menopause and menopause, and the many 'aha' moments that come with life after drop-off.

Evelyn, by all definitions, is a traditional woman. She is part of a generation of women considered trailblazers and free spirits. But if you ask her, she will tell you, she is far from being a free spirit or trailblazer. As a young woman attending Agnes Scott College in Atlanta, GA, her belief system and definition of self were closely tied to who her parents were and were not. A significant part of her life was spent living by what she called "the rules." She attended and graduated from the same college her mother attended, and like her mother, she completed her studies, receiving her BSN and MRS simultaneously; she did everything by the book and as expected of her. But at fifty-nine, her definition of self and life well-lived continues to evolve and grow in ways that force her to redefine her expectations and consider experiences that were once dreams and realities afforded the young. Feeling compelled to redefine her position in the world and use her voice to convey messages that reflect what she calls her second wind, she joined multiple Facebook groups hoping to connect with empty-nesters thriving well after drop-off.

"I am new to these kinds of groups. I've been on Facebook for a while now, more as a lurker than an active participant. A friend added me to the traveling group. I am intrigued by women who can easily book flights and travel alone to countries outside their comfort

122

zones and familiar environments. Recently, I stumbled upon a family who sold all their possessions and packed their remaining necessities to live full-time on a boat. Two parents are living and raising their two children on a boat. What a time to be alive, right?" she shared via Instant Messenger.

"Yes, times have changed; the possibilities and options seem only to be limited by our own thoughts and comfort level. What a time to be alive, indeed! Are you thinking about traveling solo?" I wrote.

"Yes, yes, I am, which is extremely unlike me. In our thirty-seven years of marriage, my husband and I have never once slept apart, not even for a night, nonetheless a weekend or entire week. Most of my online hours are spent researching the best place for first-time solo travelers' and engaging with the ladies in the group, hoping to take the leap next year in celebration of my sixtieth birthday. As I write this, all I can think is, who am I? Who is this adventurous lady making these lavish plans?" she wrote, adding the shock and smiley emojis.

"I understand your excitement; solo traveling is so liberating. How does your husband feel about your desire to travel solo?"

"He would prefer I go with a group; he doesn't like the idea of me going solo but understands my desire to go at it alone. The past few years have been challenging;

we've had many firsts and many, many losses. My last living parent died in January of this year, and last year, my husband's parents died three months apart. I am the first to admit that adjusting to life as an empty nester while going through all these life changes, and navigate the roller coaster that is menopause hasn't been easy. To live long enough to see your babies navigate life as adults is an incredible blessing. But aging is humbling. Some days I look in the mirror, and I look my age; other days I look like the crypt keeper, almost unrecognizable, like who is this woman looking back at me and what has she done to the real me?" she wrote, adding the shocked emoji.

At fifty-nine, Evelyn could easily write a book with step-by-step tips on all things skincare, health, and wellness; she exudes radiance and beauty from the inside out. But like most women living in a society where self-deprecating thoughts and words are synonymous with self-awareness and having a 'humbling' nature, she is her own worst critic.

"I wasn't prepared, and to be honest, I never thought I would be one of those women who experience empty-nest syndrome. It's like one day, I was fine, excited even, then out of nowhere, I began experiencing deep feelings of loss, nostalgia, and regret. It felt like the walls were closing in on me as life and people were quickly passing me by. I still feel like myself and am grateful for all I have experienced, but every now and then, when I look in the mirror expecting to see my old self, looking back at me is the face and demeanor of my mother and, on my worst day, my late grandmother…on her death bed!. How did I get here so quickly?! I love social media; it has given me the opportunity to meet some incredible women and get a front-row view of how they are navigating this season of adulthood. Seeing women experiencing other options for a well-lived life has been fascinating, but I must admit, I've had moments where I allowed the green-eyed monster the space to skew my perception of self and time. Seeing my age mates and some younger women navigate life unafraid, with what looks like limitless options, made me feel out of the loop and old. I know, I know, operating from a place of comparison and envy is never a good idea, but I can't help it. I often feel like I've missed the window for reinventing myself, and now, at almost sixty, time is not on my side," she said.

I sat on my response for a few minutes, not because I didn't know what to say or had positioned myself in a place of judgment, but because I knew all too well the feelings of regret, loss, and urgency Evelyn was experiencing. Like Evelyn, I believe social media to be one of the most valuable and life-changing tools of the 21st century. This book wouldn't be possible without the reach available through social media. But it is not without a truckload of downsides— comparison being one of them. It's easy to take a sixty-second or three to ten-minute video of someone sharing a win or success and think that one post is the entirety of their journey, especially when the win is something we deem unattainable or too big for us to reach or experience ourselves.

Envy is an interesting feeling. It's one of those emotions that clouds our judgment yet forces us to ask ourselves those hard questions and re-analyze our who and why. If we take the time to consider the root of those feelings, we will learn that we do not desire to have what our neighbor or age mates have, but rather, we mourn our inability to have the same level of luck and success with the perceived ease and quickness displayed on our screen. We compare our entire book of life and devalue and discount our progress and good fortune based on one or two well-curated views of small and specific pages in another's book of life.

We curse time for moving too fast while wasting it on comparisons and if only. We measure our ability to reach a goal or partake in a particular experience by the resources available to another, completely missing and pushing aside those qualities, opportunities, and gifts available to us that are, in fact, very specific to our own individual journey. We overlook the fact that, more often than not, we have exactly what we need to redefine and reinvent ourselves on our terms— if only we understood that most overnight success and reinvention of self rarely happen overnight. Curating a lifestyle that can withstand days where happiness and contentment elude you will require a mindset shift, one where time and age are not seen as a hindrance or handicap but as the fuel needed to get on the right path.

"Oh, I understand! These empty nest years can best be described as having way too much time on our hands while being constantly aware of how quickly time is moving us closer to our sunset. Feeling like you're running out of time is normal, but no matter how long we live, we will always wish for more time. I'm curious: how much time do you think you need to recreate your desired lifestyle? Because whether you push forward or remain still, time will do what it does, with or without your acceptance and understanding of its value, you know what I mean?" I asked.

"Hahaha, well, that's a loaded question. I don't know; I would like to live another twenty-five or thirty years if I'm healthy, of course, but who knows? As much as I lament over aging and feeling like I am late to the party, I am grateful to have a partner who has stood beside me through some of my most transformative years. He is the calm to my storm. The poor guy indulges all my ups and downs, new ideas, new faces (lol), and everything in between. He is my biggest supporter and pushes me to get out of the ever-looming empty-nest funk and just do it... I just need to figure out what 'it' is."

No matter how long you've had an empty nest, navigating the rollercoaster of emotions that comes with this new parenting role, all while going through the ups and downs of peri-menopause and menopause, is no easy feat. Having a community of like-minded women and nurturing a healthy partnership with your significant other is so important.

"I know my life is not over, and I have much to be grateful for and look forward to. But I struggled for a long time with defining what this phase of my life should look like. Something as simple as defining my fashion and beauty style was both challenging and awkward. I felt like a prepubescent girl at a new school, trying to find my place and voice. Understanding where I fit and how I can best use my experiences and resources to create a lifestyle that best represents my current station in life is quite the task. What advice would you give to women who, after many years as empty nesters, continue to struggle with finding their happy place?" she asked.

"Well, for one, happiness comes and goes. Don't chase happiness, but focus on creating a lifestyle that speaks to your definition of life well lived. Dig deeper to know who you are, and seek opportunities that force you to expand and experience your authentic self. When you reach the point of truly knowing and defining your who and why, share it with the world. Like you, I remember feeling anxious about my need for change; I felt I was too old to attempt any reinvention of self, and I feared those closest to me wouldn't accept my improved self. But I have learned that when we seek to improve ourselves and experience those things that we once thought were out of character or out of our reach, we soon learn that the world doesn't crumble when we think or live outside the box. We learn there are people searching and waiting for testimonials and success stories of women our age doing it their way. As the saying goes, first, they judge you and find humor in your strength and desire for an improved self and life, then they imitate you, hoping to find their own voice and meaning of a purposeful life. So, take another route, reinvent yourself as often as you need to, and show up unapologetically; I promise you, the world will adjust!"

Six months later:

"Happiest of birthdays, dear friend; I hope you're having a blast! xx", I wrote via Instant Messenger.

"Hey, my love! Thank you SO much, and yes, I am having THE absolute best birthday. Steven and I flew to Croatia, and to my surprise, the kids are here, too.

Steven charted a yacht, and we are on our second day sailing the most beautiful waters I have ever seen (can you believe it? I'm living my best boat life. Not quite the solo trip I initially wanted, but in the past six months, I've learned there is no one way to do this empty nest thing, and everything is not for everybody...and that's okay!":).

One barrier to creating your own path after drop-off that adds to the confusion of knowing your "why" is thinking life is one size fits all and what works for one person should work for all. Choosing a lifestyle after drop-off requires an open mind and the ability to admire another's life choices, all while understanding and embracing your individual needs and desires. Most of us will never feel pushed to sell all our possessions to backpack or sail through open seas; some may, and that's their beautiful journey.

Others may choose to finally turn that hobby into a career, join classes that were once an afterthought, or try as many pet projects and ideas as possible before settling for one or many. No lifestyle is right or wrong; the key is to stop chasing happiness and instead make intentional choices with the portions available to you to design a life that speaks to your individual needs and belief system and can weather the numerous highs and lows of aging. The pathways of growing older are as diverse and varied as the individuals traversing them. Embracing diversity in aging is important, as it allows us to honor the distinctiveness of our journey and shatters the societal constructs of what aging should look like. Society often imposes a rigid and linear narrative on aging - retire at a certain age, slow down, and embrace a more sedentary lifestyle. However, this standard narrative fails to consider diverse and nuanced experiences, evolving aspirations, and capabilities that individuals continue to possess as they age.

For some, aging might herald a period of newfound freedom and exploration– a time to pursue neglected passions, embark on new adventures, or even start a second career. Others might find fulfillment in dedicating time to family, volunteering, or immersing themselves in lifelong learning. The essence lies in understanding that aging isn't a one-way street but rather, a diverse landscape with multiple avenues to explore. As you look to social media for inspiration, tips, and community, understand this: no one owes you there behind the scenes. While many on social media share their authentic journeys, most good days shared on these platforms are slightly exaggerated, while most bad days are measured. Yet still, no one owes you their entire life story. Be inspired, but take the well-curated snippets for what they are, a brief moment in time shared to show good, bad, or other, nothing is everlasting, and life is not one size fits all. Comparing your journey to another or trying to fit into someone else's mold is a disservice to your individuality.

Embracing your unique qualities and acknowledging that life doesn't follow a one-size-fits-all pattern is the first step towards leading a life that resonates with your true self. Each empty nest year is like a blank canvas awaiting your personal touch. A template inviting you to grab a brush to paint your own masterpiece depicting a well-lived life. Embrace your individuality, honor your aspirations, and pursue a life that resonates with your true self. Remember, it's not about fitting into a predefined mold; it's about creating a life that reflects your passions, values, and dreams. In a world filled with ever-growing responsibilities and obligations, exploring one's passions and interests becomes a luxury and a vital necessity for a balanced and meaningful life. It is a testament to the richness and depth of life that can only be uncovered when you decide to pursue happiness on your terms, embracing the unique opportunities that midlife and life as an empty nester has to offer.

Answer these questions in your next journal entry:

- Who in your life faced a personal failure that should have broken them, yet pushed through despite it all? What do you admire most about their journey?

- What keeps you from giving up?

- How would you describe your favorite holiday?

- What one truth you learned in midlife you wished you had known earlier in life?

- You have the opportunity to speak with your ninety-year-old self; what will you thank her for?

"We have to be able to grow up. Our wrinkles are our medals of the passage of life. They are what we have been through and who we want to be."
- Lauren Hutton

Connecting The Dots

"This is one of the glories of man, the inventiveness of the human mind and the human spirit; whenever life doesn't seem to give an answer, we create one." — **Lorraine Hansberry**

May 22, 2018 — Turn Back Time — Nazare, Portugal

CAMILLE

"What encourages you to show up?" I asked. She paused and looked over to the ocean, her gaze following the progression of water from a distance. She watched as the waves unfurled, their crests glistening like diamonds in the sunlight before gently cascading down in a cascade of frothy white foam. The translucent water carried with it a murmur of stories from distant shores, secrets whispered by the winds and the currents. As I watched her take in the smell and sounds of the ocean, a sense of tranquility came over me, and the symphony of the sea filled my ears. The distant calls of seagulls seemed to blend seamlessly with the soothing rhythm of the waves, creating a soft yet rambunctious melody of nature's harmony.

The waves of North Beach (Praia do Norte), in Nazaré, Portugal, an old fishing town two hours north of Lisbon, is home to some of the biggest waves in the world, averaging about 60 feet high, but in the Winter months can occasionally reach as high as 100 feet; it is a beach lover's dream location. While a beloved gem to locals, Nazaré attracts visitors from all over the world, especially surfers and those who like to watch and experience the biggest shore waves in the world. As the waves drew nearer, I could feel the cool mist on my skin, a delicate touch of ocean breath.

Smiling at the dance between the waves and sunlight, she points toward a row of colorful wooden beach chairs meticulously placed on the sand and says, "She does, she encourages me to show up. I can't imagine my life without her or fathom an existence without her words of encouragement."

I turned my attention to where she pointed; standing near a row of colorful wooden beach chairs stood a graceful silhouette; her hair, a tapestry of silver and ash grey, cascaded down her shoulders in gentle waves. The sunlight caught in the strands, creating a shimmering halo that framed her face. As she gazed out at the horizon, the wisdom of age was evident in the way she observed the waves, a quiet acknowledgment of the ebb and flow that mirrored the cycles of life.

Her colorful sundress was a blend of tradition and practicality, a nod to her coastal heritage, with a well-worn shawl draped over her shoulders. The sea breeze played with the fringes of the shawl, creating a gentle dance between the fabric and the wind. While she stood only steps away from where we sat, she and the sea appeared to be one. The ocean's vastness held a kindred spirit, a reminder that just as the tides returned without fail, she too, had endured, adapted, and found her way back home.

I met Camille at a restaurant in Nazaré, Portugal, seated at one of the many beachfront restaurants overlooking the beach. I was tired, anxious, and questioning every decision I'd made up to this point. It was just an hour ago that I was dropped off by car service from Lisbon International Airport to a town that I had only seen on YouTube videos and blog posts. The trip from Los Angeles International Airport to Lisbon was not easy. I missed my connecting flight in Istanbul, which forced me to spend a night at Istanbul Airport.

What was supposed to be a fourteen-hour journey turned into a day and a half of travel exhaustion. By the time I arrived near my Airbnb, schlepping four pieces of luggage up and down what felt like never-ending, zig-zag staircases, my luggage and I looked like we had been to hell and back. Looking back, I am sure Camille's openness and willingness to share a bit of her story with me were largely due to the fact that, as much as I tried to put on a strong and impervious facade and as excited as I was to have made the move to Portugal, I was both tired and concerned that I may have taken on more than I can handle.

"My mother was born here in Nazare, and while she's spent most of her adult life in the States, in New Bedford, Massachusetts, her life began, and her transition will start and end here, in Nazare." I turned to look at her mother. "There's something unfinished about being an immigrant that only another immigrant or a child of one can understand. The process of immigration leaves scars that no matter how fruitful a life you have in your new home, leaving your native culture and mother tongue to settle in a new place means inevitably leaving a part of who you are behind. No matter how settled you are in your new country, there is within you a longing and nostalgia for the person you once was and curiosity of who you might have been if you stayed."

"I understand," I said, still looking at her mother admiring the ocean. Her composure seemed to merge with the rhythm of the sea. "Where do you fit in your mother's return home? Is this a permanent move for you, as well?

"Yes and no," she said, shaking her head side to side, "I don't know, to be honest. My mother returned to connect with the woman she was prior to moving to the States at nineteen and to make peace with what could have been, and I naturally came with her. I am retired, and I am her only child. My boys, thirty-four and thirty-two, have well-established careers and have built beautiful lives for themselves in New Bedford. As a widow, this move is my second wind. There's a part of me hoping my time here, whether three months or three years, will feed my desire to connect with my roots, leading to many "aha moments" that will help me connect the dots and discover who I can become. While the world would like women my age to believe we are invisible, I have a role model who, at eighty-six, continues to command each room she enters and is a walking billboard for dreaming big dreams. I grew up in a home where age alone didn't determine one's capacity to achieve new goals, learn new skills, or engage in new experiences. I know not many women my age can say as much or still have a parent who is their cheerleader while also practicing what they preach. Trust me, I don't make light of my good fortune. Which is why, no matter how long or short a time I have in Nazare, it will be a season of meaningful moments."

I could write an entire book on the clarity and visions of new life and opportunities shared during our conversation. When I sat for our conversation, I had many doubts and trepidation about my move to Portugal. As a newcomer to a new country, Camilla's story was the boost and reminder I needed to re-ignite the fire that led me to Nazare and remind me that taking chances, like moving to another city or country, even though challenging, is a risk worth taking.

"I guess I am what you'd call a seasoned empty-nester. I am well past the season to be affected by empty-nest syndrome. Yet, my desire to reinvent and redefine myself remains a significant part of my growth journey, Camille continues. Being here in Nazare grounds me. Being around women for whom aging is not something to remedy or despise is liberating. It reminds me to define aging, wellness, and self-care on my terms."

While feelings and perspectives are highly individual and can vary greatly based on personal experiences, cultural backgrounds, and individual personalities, in a world where the quest for youthfulness is masked as wellness, societal pressures and unrealistic beauty standards often drive the quest, perpetuating an unattainable ideal that undermines genuine self-care and inner well-being.

This constant evolution and redefining of aging requires a mindset that embraces aging outside societal expectations and age-related biases. Your journey of self-discovery, growth, and empowerment must be self-defined, with the gusto to do it your way, with or without societal validation and acceptance. Which can help redefine the narrative of what aging is and is not.

But reinvention is not merely a response to societal shifts; it is a conscious choice to embrace change and seize the reins of one's destiny. Whether forty-five or seventy-five, we must refrain from viewing age as a limitation but more so as a springboard to explore uncharted territories and rediscover the depths of our potential. We must trust our gut and the accumulation of wisdom and life experiences that we've gathered over the years to serve as a solid foundation for reinvention. Each triumph, setback, and lesson learned along the way serves as a treasure trove of knowledge, providing valuable insights that can guide new ventures and position us to experience life with new eyes.

For far too long, age has been mistakenly equated to stagnation, limitation, and sadness. By leaning into knowledge that can only be gained through life experiences, seasoned empty nesters can challenge these stereotypes and demonstrate that life is not a linear trajectory but a series of exciting chapters waiting to be written. This act of self-discovery will guide you to reconnect with your passions, revive long-lost interests, and explore new horizons that align with your evolving sense of self.

In today's rapidly changing world, adaptability is a prized trait. Embracing reinvention cultivates resilience and flexibility, attributes that will make it easier to thrive in the face of challenges. Having an openness to reinvention will equip you with the ability to navigate new technologies, adapt to shifting work environments, and engage with younger generations in meaningful ways. This adaptability not only enriches personal experiences but also contributes to the broader tapestry of intergenerational connections and knowledge exchange. Reinvention catalyzes a sense of purpose that is often heightened in the later stages of life. Whether pursuing a second career, engaging in philanthropy, or embarking on creative endeavors, fostering a positive outlook can propel you to continue making meaningful contributions to your communities and society.

Of course, embracing reinvention is not without its challenges. Fear of the unknown and the comfort of familiarity can be formidable barriers. However, these challenges are opportunities for personal growth. Overcoming them reinforces resilience, fosters a growth mindset, and inspires a profound sense of accomplishment that can only come from surmounting obstacles. This transformative path holds the promise of rediscovering passions, nurturing growth, challenging societal norms, and finding renewed purpose.

Embracing reinvention will empower you to shatter limitations and seize the vibrant tapestry of possibilities that life has to offer. As you continue to navigate this chapter, you're not only redefining your own narratives but will inspire future generations to embrace the indomitable spirit of reinvention. Fight the urge to make light of your strengths and experiences. Acknowledge your accomplishments and the experiences that have shaped you into the person you are today. Acknowledge and take pride in those skills, knowledge, and wisdom that you possess, which are valuable assets regardless of age. Shift your focus from limitations to possibilities. I am sure you've heard of or have met people in your own life who have achieved remarkable wins much later in life; refer to those people and stories when in need of inspiration.

Continuous learning and personal growth go hand-in-hand. Enroll in that class, workshop, or online course that aligns with your interests or offers opportunities for skill development. Don't feel rush to get to the finish line. This is not a marathon or competition; it is your race, your pace. No matter your interest or desire for improvement set achievable short-term and long-term goals that align with your passions and aspirations.

While meeting new people can be challenging as we age, surround yourself with a supportive network of friends, family, and peers who uplift and motivate you. Never feel guilty for blocking, deleting, and moving away from those who come to steal your joy or put you in a box based on their idea of what "women of a certain age" should or shouldn't be.

Challenge negative self-talk. Learn your triggers so you may easily identify and challenge any negative self-talk or self-limiting beliefs related to age. Keep a journal of moments, people, or things that trigger those thoughts and reframe these thoughts into more positive and empowering narratives. Celebrate your successes and milestones, no matter how small they might seem. Recognize your achievements and get comfortable with sharing them out loud. Document them in a journal to reference on days when you doubt your abilities or need a reminder of your strengths and ingenuity.

Shout it from the mountaintop. When you experience wins or overcome challenges that you once thought were impossible due to age or perceived lack, share it with women in your circle, on and offline. So many of us live with limiting beliefs because we do not see people who look like us, are our age-mates, or are of similar backgrounds living outside the norm or doing life their way. Be open to showing others that there are other alternatives to aging that go beyond what they see in their immediate circle.

Whether on or offline, the resources available to help reshape your perspective on aging are invaluable. Buy the books, subscribe to podcasts that speak to your needs, and follow social media accounts offering authentic tips and experiences for people in this season of life. But remember, at some point, you're going to have to put down the book, turn off the podcast, and bring what you are learning to reality.

Answer these questions in your next journal entry:

- What have been the most significant lessons you've learned about love and relationships?

- What have you learned about forgiveness and letting go that impacts your who and why?

- What boundaries do you establish to ensure individual autonomy and maintain a healthy balance between independence and togetherness?

- Finish this sentence, my children would be shocked to know_____.

- Share one treasured experience from different phases of your life that you wish to experience again.

"You've got to learn to leave the table when love's no longer being served." — *Nina Simone*

PART FOUR
Party of One

Divorce/Separation in an Empty Nest

"All too often women believe it is a sign of commitment, an expression of love, to endure unkindness or cruelty, to forgive and forget. In actuality, when we love rightly we know that the healthy, loving response to cruelty and abuse is putting ourselves out of harm's way." — *bell hooks*

July 27, 2012 — Dr. Elizabeth Jacobs — Long Island City, New York

Dr. Jacobs: Were your expectations of marriage reasonable?

I met Dr. Jacobs at a fundraising event in Long Island City, New York. She was one of many healthcare professionals invited to speak on the intersectionality of trauma. While there were hundreds of women in attendance, every word, analogy, and experience she shared felt like a direct acknowledgment of my past and a gentle, nudging call to action. Speaking on the lasting effects of child abuse (both physical and psychological), i.e., self-imposed social isolation, imposter syndrome, and codependency, I knew if anyone could help me get to the other side of why not me? It would be her.

I am not new to therapy, at least not the thought of it. Seeking therapy, or rather, needing therapy, was something I've heard talked about since my early pre-teen years. As a ten-year-old in the fifth grade, I spent a lot of time volunteering in the assistant principal's office. The volunteer desk was very well situated. My desk placed me in direct view of the nurse's office, where I could easily hear all types of student and family drama. It was the perfect setup for those who love to stay in the know(translation: mini busy-body). To this day, I remember clearly the voice of our school nurse, Mildred, saying to the assistant principal, "This one is going to need some serious therapy when s/he's older," referring to yet another child acting up or being "sassy." Therapy was brought up so often that I was convinced it was an expected part of adulting. While I never got called to the principal's office for bad behavior and was able to keep the effects of my trauma inward, I knew therapy was definitely in my future.

As a child, hearing that other children are experiencing similar dysfunction or situations worse than what you are experiencing normalizes trauma and abuse, making it appear to be an integral part of the family unit. The thing about sharing trauma stories as children is that one can easily grow to accept and expect dysfunctional behavior as part of one's overall life experience. To a ten-year-old, those experiences can easily be seen as normal and acceptable, a rite of passage of sorts.

As adults, when we share our pain with others, we seek to normalize open conversations on trauma, injustice, and abuse, setting the stage for change and reformation. But for children, pain bonding is not done to illicit change but to somehow convince each other of its normalcy. It's much easier to rationalize and make sense of hurt and pain when we know others have or are experiencing the same; it creates a sort of dysfunctional sisterhood, where one tries to outdo the other on whose experience is worse. Pain or trauma boding isn't something that happens out of nowhere in adulthood; for many, like myself, it began in childhood and continued when choosing my now ex-husband. If you're looking for the recipe for a doomed marriage, it's one part trauma bonding, one part naiveté, and two parts holding the person in front of you to expectations that only the person you created in your head can live up to.

Be grateful—it could always be worse.

Like most people raised in challenging homes, learning to accurately define gratitude vs. acceptance is quite liberating. I remember it like it was yesterday; I was sitting at my assigned desk in the assistant principal's office when nurse Mildred rushed past me, speaking to AP Henry, "You're needed upfront; it seems the twins will no longer be on our roster," she said. The twins are a set of boys known by faculty as double trouble. If one is sent to the principal's office, the other is never too far behind. While I didn't know the details of their situation, I, like the rest of the fifth-grade class, knew they were in foster care, or as Mildred called them, "children of the system." From the bits I could hear of the conversation, it seemed the twins had finally found parents willing to adopt them, "This is their fourth family," whispered Mildred, "God bless whoever is willing to take on that load. You couldn't pay me enough to babysit those two; nonetheless, adopt them," she continued. Leading assistant principal Henry through the door, she turned to me and said, "You should be grateful you have parents who love you. That's not always the case for a lot of children."

To this day, I remain perplexed by the idea that children should be grateful for parents who do what parents are supposed to do. It is as if keeping a child safe, fed, and warm is the epitome of goodness and good parenting. Mildred knew nothing of my life at home. All she knew was what I allowed her to know and see. I presented well. In my household, appearance was everything, so my hair was always done, clothes well-fitted, pressed, and proper. I was taught early to always keep all family business at home, and when push comes to shove, you close your nose and drink up.

I didn't answer Mildred, I gave her my signature one-sided smile while rubbing the inside of my palm. The older I got, the less grateful I felt about my situation. Did I accept the cards dealt to my parents? Absolutely. Am I grateful they didn't play them as badly as other parents? Absolutely not.

If ever I am asked to share one thing that stands out in my healing journey, it would be this— you can accept and make peace with a person's maltreatment of you and forgive their ignorance without feeling pushed to show gratitude or be grateful because it could have been worse. Worse is subjective; one person's "this test is a learning opportunity" is another person's last straw.

It took three months to book my first therapy session with Dr. Jacobs, what was supposed to be a couple of sessions here and there turned into five years of life-changing sessions that will forever be part of my best years of growth and healing. The first year of therapy was spent understanding my role in the demise of my marriage. Each session started with a question, and out of the fifty-two questions asked of me that first year, one question remains the building block for all relationships:

Are your expectations reasonable?

Expectations vs. reality

No one enters marriage intending to divorce; I at least didn't. I was raised by a single mother who parent with an iron fist that was fueled by a gross misunderstanding of God and the Holy Bible. We, by all definitions, were devout Christians, Pentecostals to be exact. From a very young age, my understanding of marriage was that good, bad, or other, it is a union only to be broken by death. I, for a long time, agreed with this ideology. Especially since, as the oldest of four children, I saw firsthand the shunning and shaming experienced by single mothers. The degrading and demeaning manner in which Christians speak to and about single mothers and their children is enough to drive one to atheism.

No one understands (or even acknowledges) the social stigma that exists for single moms unless you are, in fact, a single mom, or the eldest child forced to play nice in an environment where the privilege to be seen and treated as a child, is strongly tied to the misfortunes of your single parent. Sunday service was a combination of hypocritical praise and harmful judgment, all under the guise of upholding misconstrued biblical standards and practices. Disapproving looks and snares rang just as loud as prayers for grace and mercy. From a very young age, I vowed that if and when I married, it would be forever. I was determined not to be another statistic and, in many ways, redeem my mother's name by upholding principles and standards that represent holiness and respectability.

At nineteen, I met my now ex-husband at church and had two daughters by the time I was twenty-seven. To say we grew apart is an understatement. Looking back, our relationship was one of convenience, trauma bonding, and situation-ship. He provided me with a way out of an abusive environment, and I fed his need for control and possessiveness. I shared too much, while he shared just enough to get me hooked. I believed in complete transparency, while he practiced selective transparency, giving me just enough to see him as my saving grace but not enough to see the price attached to him "saving" me.

I expected a savior but got a sergeant instead. It was a relationship doomed from our first hello, but one I needed to experience to learn when and how to say goodbye. It would be easy to place all blame and misunderstandings at the foot of my ex, but as someone who grew up too fast, where much was expected of me, with very little guidance or care of my needs and feelings, I was, in all matters of marriage, and by all definitions, a child playing dress-up.

I entered marriage with enough baggage and pain to challenge even the strongest union. From the beginning of our relationship, I vowed to be the wife and mother my mother never was. I knew how to be a mother, I mothered my siblings and was a role model to many younger children in my community. I held close to the vision of who I wished my mother was and had scars both externally and internally to refer to when deciding what works and what doesn't work when attempting to raise and nourish a young mind.

But like most women who grew up having to fill adult shoes— cooking, cleaning, playing mother to younger siblings, by the time you have your own family, you are not only tired, but you still seek to feed, protect, and give voice to the little girl inside you still in need of nurturing and recognition. I wanted, no, needed my husband to not only understand this sentiment but also provide me the space and support to indulge that side of myself, as I was, in many ways, re-writing my childhood. Therapy helped me take ownership of my role in the demise of my marriage. Each session were little seeds planted to later reveal new growth or neglected leaves. Looking back, my innate desire to be loved, validated, and heard were contributing factors to the admirable and lovable characteristics most praised and favored by my ex-husband— adaptable, easygoing, non-confrontational, and selfless. Those characteristics were loved and admired by many, but they were not to my benefit, as they were rooted and nurtured in pain and neglect.

I was easygoing because I learned early to stifle my voice and dismiss my wants and desires as the big picture never included my overall well-being.

I was non-confrontational because I desperately needed and wanted to be liked, even if it meant putting up with things that were both inappropriate and dehumanizing. I adapted well to change as consistency and definitive plans were never part of my upbringing; being able to easily go with the flow and adjust as needed was a must in my childhood home.

Sometimes, as it was in my case, our most admired qualities are admirable because they benefit others more than they benefit us. My ex was intentional in his care of my daughters and me. He studied me well and spoke to my pain in ways that were not to my benefit, which prolonged the possibility of addressing and healing those pain points. My need for validation empowered him, as I was easily moldable and would rise and fold according to his feelings and thoughts of me. You see, the thing about young love and marrying young is that, more often than not, one partner will consciously or unconsciously assume the role of parent, leaving the other to determine expectations that are abusive vs. behavior and expectations that are supposed to be part of a healthy marriage.

I knew what abuse looked like; I knew when she entered the room and could sense her presence before she made her presence known. Abuse, even when silent, is loud, overpowering, and commanding. It demands attention and forces you to acknowledge your worth or lack thereof. I knew how to respond to abuse and learned quickly how to react and protect myself from its wrath. But love, love in the context of marriage, was new to me. I knew how to fall in love, as the only requirement for falling in love is the belief that the one who catches your fall will elevate you to heights that you're unable to bring yourself to on your own. Love in the context of needing to be saved is the complete opposite of things needed to build and maintain a healthy marriage. My first love set the stage and, to this day, is part of the blueprint I refer to when deciding who gets a front-row seat in my life.

While our marriage ended in divorce, I learned firsthand that young love, with all its beauty, can condition us to accept behaviors that are not only harmful but feed into fears that become the catalyst for enduring years of unrealistic and unhealthy attachment styles. I didn't wait until my daughters graduated high school to leave my ex; I knew immediately after having my second child that I had fallen too deep and needed to prepare my exit plan. I no longer needed saving, at least not by a mere man. There is no golden rule on when to stay or when to go; choosing to leave a marriage is never black or white. My decision to leave when I did doesn't make my choice any better than someone choosing to stay until their child(ren) graduates high school. What's important to understand is that, whether you leave when they are young or older, your children will have their own interpretation of your marriage and parenting style; this love story, although it started with only two people, will be examined and retold by many, with your children sharing their own version.

It wasn't until I started writing this book that I learned of the astonishingly high rate at which couples seek divorce once their children have left the nest. Empty nest divorce is not only common once the last child has left the nest, but researchers have found that for couples who end up divorcing after drop-off, the idea of divorce was always part of their endgame. For many, children are the glue keeping the marriage together. As once children are removed from the equation, and parents no longer have the ups and downs of raising young children to distract them and fill voids, all underlying problems in their marriage become unavoidable and paramount. As a single empty nester, I'm often asked to share what I've learned thus far on this journey; the answers are simple yet life-changing.

Tips to remember while going through this season:

Give yourself permission to feel all the emotions that come with accepting your new role as a single parent to young adult children. Allow yourself the space and grace to feel the fear and anxiety that comes with divorce. Vocalize it; your hurt matters and your disappointment is understandable. Put a name to your pain, and let it run its course. I found journaling at that time in my life to be immensely therapeutic. As I look back at some of my writings and thought processes during that time, I realize that many of the scenarios that I thought would come to break me never happened. And the things that did come to break me are now the stepping stones I use to determine my next steps. So, do yourself a favor and write it out; your future self will thank you.

It's perfectly okay and acceptable to feel regret, sadness, and loss. What is not okay is keeping those feelings inward for fear of judgment or being misunderstood. Those who love you and want what's best for you will not only understand but will show you so much grace that their love and understanding will help you make sense of it all. Fight the urge to grieve in isolation, lean on those who love you, and give yourself grace. This season is not the all of you and does not define your entire existence.

No matter their age, your child(ren) can feel and see your pain; don't try to hide it. Divorce (although none of us marry or get into a relationship thinking of worse-case scenarios), should be talked about as openly and candidly as you would any other topic. How you deal with your partner, yourself, and your children during this time will forever be part of their childhood memories. If you do nothing else, allow your children to see the human side of you. Trust me, they can handle it.

It's easy to get so consumed in processing the changes that are taking place in your life that you push aside building a solid relationship with your child(ren), thinking you'll get to them when things are better or settled down a bit. While separation/divorce proceedings can go on for a long time, they are not everlasting; all have an end date. But the bond you create with your child(ren) during this time will play a significant role in how they communicate and interact with you once it's over. Keep that in mind while going through what may appear to be the most challenging time of your life. Give yourself some grace. You are not unlovable, unworthy, incapable, or any other belittling term being thrown at you by others or the little voice inside of you. You are not defined by the mistakes of your past; your mistakes are not the whole of you.

Don't let anyone, yourself included, convince you otherwise. Move with grace, openness, and willingness to discard that which no longer adds value to your vision of a well-lived life. You're worth it! And your best days are most certainly not behind you. When deciding your next steps, move with facts. Your financial stability is just as important as your mental and emotional stability. Women are often hit harder financially by divorce, making it harder to get back on our feet when it's over. Plan and move strategically. If you're in the beginning stages of planning to leave your marriage, take some time to get organized and educated.

Ensure you have access to and copies of pay stubs, bills, credit card and bank statements, mortgage statements, investment statements, and income tax papers. If your husband initiated the divorce and is now hiding important financial documents from you, make a note of all that you remember: bills, debts, and assets. Even if you don't have exact amounts, make note of them anyway, as your attorney will be able to request financial disclosure, but having a general picture will help you start planning.

Any joint credit cards and loans in both names are the responsibility of both spouses. To avoid a situation where your spouse runs a large balance on a joint credit card and refuses to pay, take your name off all joint credit card accounts. If you're in a community property state, any loans in both names will be joint and split 50/50. Ensure you have at least one credit card in your name and get separate checking and savings accounts. For many, having a plan can sometimes be a luxury; it's not always possible to have a perfect plan. But be aware of what you have and the resources available to you. It goes without saying that your safety and that of your children is of primary importance; explore all resources to ensure your safety and that of your children.

Going through a divorce can be an incredibly challenging and emotionally draining experience. A process that may evoke feelings of fear and shame. Allow yourself the freedom to grieve and make peace with the roller coaster of feelings associated with this experience. This chapter of your life does not define you; if you allow it, divorce can be a stepping stone to new beginnings. Your worth isn't tethered to a relationship status. Embrace the fact that you are a multifaceted individual with remarkable strengths and capabilities. Embrace this transition as a chance to reclaim your independence, rediscover your passions, and nurture the aspects of your life that bring you joy and fulfillment.

Make it a priority to surround yourself with friends, family, or professionals who understand and uplift you during this time. Lean on them for comfort and guidance. Practice self-compassion and prioritize self-care. Take small steps each day toward healing and rebuilding. Reflect on your experiences and use them as lessons that contribute to your growth. Celebrate your resilience and courage as you navigate this challenging period. Remember, this phase does not diminish your value and strength; rather, they are magnified as you embrace your journey toward a brighter, more empowered future. You are capable, resilient, and deserving of a life filled with happiness and fulfillment. Keep moving forward with grace, and know that you have the strength within you to overcome this chapter and emerge stronger, with more clarity on those things that speak to your definition of life well lived.

Answer these questions in your next journal entry:

☐ What have you learned from your child that has enriched your own life?

☐ Finish this sentence: if my life were a movie, it would be called _____.

☐ How will you continue to support and maintain a meaningful relationship with your children after they move out?

☐ If reincarnation is real, I want to come back as____, why?

☐ What role do hobbies or passions play in your life?

"It takes courage to grow up and become who you really are." — *E.E. Cummings*

Single and Ready to Mingle

"Being deeply loved by someone gives you strength while loving someone deeply gives you courage." —*Lao Tau*

June 28, 2017 — Summer of Love — Gouda, the Netherlands

ELISE

One of the first people I met when I moved to the Netherlands was a woman named Elise. Elise is a single mother to three daughters and lives in Gouda, a Dutch city south of Amsterdam, in the province of South Holland. We were online friends for five years before meeting in "real life." She and her husband separated in early 2004; divorce proceedings took what she called a lifetime and a half. While she wished her daughters had witnessed a healthy relationship between her and her ex, she knew dating would not be part of her immediate future. Even after many years of being divorced, she had no desire to date, nonetheless, marry again. The first five

166

years as a single parent were tough, with many instances where sadness and regret felt suffocating, coupled with moments of immense fear and uncertainty; child-rearing was her main priority. We met for cocktails at a cafe in the center of Gouda, cafe 1983 Gouda.

"They have so much time," said Elise, looking at a table to the right of ours, where three young women, who look to be in their early twenties, sat. I turned to look at the young women, all with their cellphones in hand, taking pictures of their orders, laughing, and sharing tips on the best way to capture images of their drinks and meals.

I smiled, and a picture of my daughters came to mind. For just a second, I thought about the role motherhood plays in how we see ourselves and define ourselves as women, women responsible for shaping the minds of young daughters.

"I know that sounds morbid and envious, but I'm not; I'm not envious at all. It's just, I don't know, I wasted so much time," she said.

I waited, trying to take in what she shared. "It's been nearly sixteen years since the divorce. The girls are thirty-two, twenty-eight, and twenty-three. All have lives outside of our mother/daughter relationship, which is fine, of course, but here I am, having wasted my prime years in marriage, followed by five years living in a perpetual pity party after the divorce; I am single, and don't know the first thing about dating at my age, where did the time go?"

I knew exactly what she was going through as I, too, put romantic desires on the back burner to focus on raising my daughters. Divorce does not only break the family unit but can also break your spirit, and if you let it, it strips you of the desire to feel and connect with another person in the most human way. Even the most amicable divorce will leave scars of self-doubt and insecurity. One of the many challenges of parenting after divorce, especially when you're the primary caretaker, is finding the right balance between motherhood and honoring your sexual and emotional needs. As honorable as it may seem to fully devote yourself to your children, completely neglecting your own needs can negatively impact the trajectory of your personal life for years to come.

"I don't even know if I can connect with a man as I did with my ex. I haven't grown hard or cold; it's just, how do I say this? It's like my light switch is stuck at one level. I would like to date again, but times have changed so much, I wouldn't know where to begin," she continued. I joined her in turning my head to look at the other patrons coming in and out of the cafe, many of whom looked to be under thirty. From the outside looking in, they all appeared to have so much time and, from a purely ageist view, so many options.

"It's funny, not haha funny, but perplexing funny, my ex met his now-wife within a year of our divorce, and much to my surprise, is still married," she said, still looking at people coming in and out of the cafe.

I smiled in acknowledgment of her comment, especially the last part. Like her ex, my ex met someone and married pretty quickly after our divorce, and from the little bit I know about him, he and his wife are going pretty strong. This type of scenario is neither new nor surprising; it's quite the norm, actually.

Most men not only move on quickly after divorce, but they, more often than not, find women who will accept and entertain long-term relationships with them despite their shortcomings. Creating a mindset where they don't feel inspired to improve themselves in preparation for a new relationship, as their mere existence and show of interest, no matter how lackluster, is enough to grab the attention and hearts of most woman on their radar.

Men will divorce and almost immediately find someone willing to accept them as they are, while women must recreate themselves and appear as perfect as humanly possible to entertain the most basic man, which, to some women, can feel like punishment for leaving a bad marriage. Ask any divorced woman about her desire to date, and she'll immediately share a laundry list of things she must correct, perfect, and heal from before she sees herself worthy of one date, nonetheless, a relationship that could lead to marriage. While most men begin losing their hair as early as thirty-two to thirty-five, can't keep a satisfying erection after forty-five, and aren't able to provide a new woman the same or similar lifestyle they offered their first family, their asks and expectations of women are both unrealistic and insanely audacious. Yet, still, they are never without viable options.

"I don't necessarily need a man, at least not in the traditional sense," Elise continues. "But I would like to feel alive again, bring life to that area of my life. As my mother would say, 'I'm hungry but far from famished.' I miss having someone to bounce ideas off of and share the ups and downs of my day. And boy, do I miss the touch of a man. Maybe it's menopause; who knows? I haven't felt this need in a while. It's like my sex drive was on pause for what seems like forever, and then, out of nowhere, hot flashes were replaced with a desire to be ravished. My ex used to rest his hand on the small of my back when we walked, making circular motions, as if to soothe my anxieties and let me know he has my back; I am ready to feel that kind of connection again."

The dating world can look very different for women over fifty. Whether it's returning after a long period of not dating or trying to work romance into established routines, understanding that dating is not what it was fifteen or even ten years ago is the first step in creating a plan to meet a compatible partner and possibly experience a long-term connection. While dating preferences differ from woman to woman, and the do's and don'ts of dating are ever-changing, whether you're looking for long-term, short-term, or seasonal relationships, we can all agree that having a diverse method for meeting a potential partner is key.

Even though dating apps remain one of the easiest ways to connect and meet a potential partner, nothing beats good old-fashioned meet-ups while doing those things you enjoy. No matter your interests, your chances of meeting a partner increase significantly when you diversify your methods for meeting and connecting with a potential partner, especially if you're a woman over fifty. The pool may be smaller, but there is no shortage of compatible partners for those who understand the pool and their pull.

Diversifying your dating portfolio and going where you are loved is advice given to women as a guide for finding a compatible partner. While both are good advice and can widen one's dating pool, engaging in activities you have no genuine interest in is never a good idea. You will appear desperate and a poser, two things that can lead to you meeting people who will try to take advantage of your need for a partner.

There is a significant difference between trying new activities that are outside of one's comfort zone for the sake of learning and genuine interest versus engaging in and pretending to enjoy an activity just for the sake of meeting a potential partner. It is impossible to attract a compatible partner while posing as something or someone you are not. Compatibility is crucial when dating over fifty. Compatibility is the measuring stick used to determine shared values, interests, goals, and ways of interacting.

Men are very simple creatures, with most incapable of seeing women as evolving, multi-faceted beings. If they meet you at a shooting range, and you pretend to enjoy a day at the range, they will assume that is an activity you genuinely enjoy and will gauge compatibility on that one activity. So, if you don't genuinely enjoy an activity, do not pretend to enjoy it for the sake of pulling a man.

Whether physical appearance, leisure activity, or lifestyle, who you say you are and present as during the first meeting and subsequent dates thereafter is the person they expect you to be the entirety of the relationship. So when in doubt, show up as your authentic self. Quite frankly, if you are a woman over twenty, whether romantic or platonic, pretending to be something you are not for the sake of connecting and keeping a relationship is truly for the birds.

If you've spent even an hour perusing dating apps, you will realize that most people do not get wiser with age. When engaging in conversation or activities with a potential partner, never assume an older person or a person closer to your age is a good catch because of age. On the contrary, most men over fifty are more confused and indecisive at fifty than in their twenties.

Meet them where they are now, not where you want them to be or should be for someone their age. While the internet creates a false sense of security and provides its users with a platform to say and do things they would never say or do in "real life" (at least not during the first few days of dating), their online persona is never too far off and, in truth, a significant part of their character.

Yes, people are layered, and it takes time to gauge true character, but common decency, respect, and kindness should not be a guessing game. You're either kind or you're not. You're either respectful or you're not. When interacting with anyone online, use the same determining factors used to gauge compatibility offline as you would online. Do not give anyone a pass under the guise of nervousness. The internet is like alcohol; both give its users the high and false confidence to openly say and share feelings that, no matter how vile and unconventional, are the user's true feelings and representation of their character. The internet offers its users the ability to exchange ideas, experiences, and desires with multiple potentials simultaneously, giving people a false sense of their pool and their pull. Just because you have the reach doesn't mean you will have access, something most people don't consider since new potentials are only a click away, or so they think.

Don't agree to activities or lifestyles that are outside of your comfort zone out of fear of missing out on a perceived great catch. Whether online or offline, when people show you who they are, don't try to dissect, pretty up, or rationalize their behavior; believe them and use that information to determine your next steps.

Never hang your cloak higher than your reach.

It's important to be mindful and have a realistic view of the pool and your pull so you can govern your expectations wisely and not waste time with people who are outside your compatibility bucket.

What is knowing your pool?

As women of a certain age, the older we get, the smaller our pool of like-minded, age-appropriate, sane, and healthy men gets. Understanding what you are working with in terms of numbers will help you have a more realistic view of dating and relationships and not waste time with incompatible people or pass over a good catch due to FOMO (fear of missing out); thinking something better is out there.

That's not to say one should date from a place of scarcity, but understanding the numbers is helpful in determining how fast or slow to move with potential partners. Most "good" men over forty-five are, in fact, married, and no sane woman is giving up on a "good" man, even when minor (sometimes major) hiccups occur. The pool of over forty-five-year-old eligible men can fill four buckets:

- those who are divorced for a good reason and should stay single
- those looking for a nurse-mate
- those who are non-committal and see dating like a kid in a candy store
- followed by a sprinkle of actual good catches who, like you, are trying to date based on values and expectations from a time that no longer exists…and they are not at the so-called hotspots everyone talks about.

Yes, there are 7+ billion people in the world, and all you need is one, but when it comes to compatibility, only a very small fraction of that number are healthy, unproblematic, generous, and sound people worth compromising your peace for or share a meal with, let alone your life. Understanding your pool and navigating accordingly is a must when dating in your fifties and beyond, as it provides a realistic view of what's out there. I meet women daily who desire to date but do so without a plan or understanding of the pool for women over fifty. We live in a time where frivolous dating is not only a waste of time but can have dangerous repercussions from a safety and health standpoint. Statistically, women over fifty are more vulnerable to contracting HIV and other sexually transmitted diseases, as they tend to let their guards down with new sexual partners and don't make a fuss about using protection since pregnancy is a nonissue. For women coming out of long-term marriages/relationships who may not have had a lot of sexual and/or dating experiences prior to marriage, this season can feel like playing catch-up, where they believe time is running out on them, evoking feelings of wanting to engage as many people as possible before "it's too late." But more doesn't necessarily mean best, and timing is everything. You can meet the next love of your life while walking out of divorce court or be in the dating field for years and never meet anyone worthy of having space in your life. No matter your intentions or preparedness plan, what's for you will not pass you by, and sadly, what is not for you will not find you.

For most women, it's not that they are not date-able or haven't dated enough, but that they have yet to meet anyone worthy of the love they are capable of giving. While others do not have a clear idea of what they want in their next relationship. Approach dating as you would any other experience you wish to have. You wouldn't relocate to a country across the globe or another city without understanding the dos and don'ts of the people and culture there, would you? The same rule applies to dating. Market research is a must. Be clear about the type of person you wish to share your time with, even if it is for short-term dating. Where does he live, what activities does he enjoy that mirror those you enjoy, and what would his day and weekend look like? What about his temperament, leadership style, and problem-solving style? You must have clear answers to these questions before considering a person dateable. Not to mention, accepting that dating has evolved greatly since you were last actively seeking a partner is vital. Attention spans are nonexistent, audacity is at an all-time high, while kindness, compassion, and common decency are at a steady decline. The pool you swam in your twenties no longer exists, as those men are either married, dead, or late in life bi/homosexual.

Move with clarity, knowing exactly who you are and what joy looks like in your life. Men rarely compromise or give grace based on love or compatibility. They stick to what they want, and while they may engage someone outside of their vision of an ideal partner, they will not commit and will not provide you with the experience you deserve, no matter how much you tweak, pull, tuck, and change yourself to fit their ideal person.

Stick to your standards and requirements; you are not dating from a place of trying to beat the fertility clock or wanting marriage for the sake of showing family and friends that you, too, have a partner. This season is about experiencing people, things, and activities that meet your criteria for a well-lived life. Fight the urge to compromise for the sake of compromising. It will not benefit you to compromise and accept behavior and lifestyles that are outside of your comfort zone, all for the sake of being in a relationship. Compromise is a vital part of all relationships, but you must have a clear definition of what it looks like for you in this current season of your life.

Agreeing to cook at home now and then when cooking is not something you enjoy is a healthy compromise. Attending an event that you may not have an interest in is a healthy compromise. Alternating between families during the holidays is, again, a healthy compromise. Any expectation that causes you to lose sight of who you are and your core values, decreases your quality of life and is not reciprocal is the opposite of healthy compromise and a healthy relationship.

What is knowing your pull?

Similarly to other service-based online spaces, a dating app is a marketplace people use to shop for people. If we are honest with ourselves, we'll all agree that we judge and compare people by how handsome, sexy, "hot," and tall they are more than we focus on and compare their character. Yes, no one can read character from a few pictures or the first introduction, but understand this: when it comes to the exterior, do not ask or seek from others what you can't be or deliver yourself.

Most near-perfect, handsome, and put-together people are not only sought after, but they, too, are looking for people who mirror and match them in both physical presentation and lifestyle. Yes, they are outliers; there are instances where opposites attract, where two people you would never think to be a pair meet and have a beautiful and healthy relationship, but that is the exception, not the rule. Let's not operate from a place of thinking that we are special unicorns who can change a person's mind about their chosen lifestyle; instead, we should accept things and people as they are and adjust our strategy and expectations accordingly. When determining your ideal partner, ask yourself, am I seeking and asking for that which I can provide, as well? Do you have the pull?

When it comes to the exterior, a fit, reasonably handsome, sexy (by your definition) man will want someone with a similar mindset and lifestyle. Most incredibly handsome and successful men who have kept up with their health will wish to have the hottest women they can pull on their arms. And, as stated above on maturity, when it comes to finding a partner, most men over fifty are regressing to their fraternity years, with a college, some high school mindset, where they date to impress their peers and prove they can still pull the hottest women available.

They date for the approval of their peers, which means they want to date women their guy friends will want to sleep with. So, before you swipe right on that really handsome, tall, seemingly successful man, ask yourself, can I meet his expectations? Do we share a similar lifestyle? And before you swipe left on the less attractive man, with the face and physique needing time to grow to love because he's well, average, ask yourself, is he more my speed? When it comes to dating, experiment always, have fun, and be open to all possibilities, but move with a good grasp of reality and understanding of who you are now, not who you wish to be or working on yourself to become.

As women, we are willing to date someone with potential (sometimes to our demise), offering grace when we should offer judgment; don't expect men to extend the same. Men see you for who you are now, not who you're working on yourself to become. If you feel who you are now doesn't match the type of men you deserve or dream of experiencing, take time to work on those things that will position you to meet and comfortably engage your type. But don't make a career out of fixing yourself. Men, with all their grand asks, are not out here getting penile enlargements, second or third streams of income, or working on past traumas to present as a well-rounded individual. They operate from a "what you see is what you get" mindset. That's not to say you, too, should operate from such a mindset. Put your best foot forward; who knows, the improvements you make to become a more engaged partner can be the catalyst to you living your best life with or without a partner.

Which is something to consider. What if you don't meet the next love of your life? Are you okay with experiencing short-term relationships or casual dating? For most people, finding a compatible partner for a long-term relationship or marriage may be a thing of the past. And it has nothing to do with their value or worth. If you are in the market desiring to meet a compatible partner, it's important to come to terms and curate a life where you are well, with or without Mr. Right. Not because you're a bad person, undateable or unworthy of love, but because dating and marriage are not what they were fifteen years ago, never mind five years ago. As a society, our attention spans are like that of a three-year-old, and the internet has convinced us that access and reach are one and the same; we overlook people in our immediate circle who could make good partners, due to FOMO and perceived access. Not to mention, definitions of love and relationship are ever-changing and expanding, and we have taken "if a man thinks it so, he is" way too literal and much too far. While it's important to remain hopeful and move with a mindset that anything is possible, creating a life that isn't solely reliant on happiness and joy derived from a relationship is essential for personal growth and fulfillment.

While companionship can certainly enhance our lives, placing all our hopes and expectations for happiness solely on a romantic partnership can be limiting. A life well lived encompasses various aspects beyond just being in a relationship. It involves nurturing individual passions, pursuing personal goals, and finding contentment within oneself. Enhancing our ability to contribute positively to relationships if and when they happen. Remain hopeful and put your best foot forward if companionship is one of your desires, but do so while building a life where you are content and experiencing life to the fullest, with or without a partner.

One can't speak about dating in midlife without including the financial aspect of dating at this stage of life, as it is quite different from dating when under fifty. Realistically, most men over fifty coming out of divorce or long-term relationships, where children are involved or have shared assets and investments with a previous partner(s), are re-entering the dating scene with much less capital. Unless he is a very well-to-do man or someone who is extremely responsible and careful with his finances, most men do not have the financial reach to give a second wife/partner the same or similar lifestyle given to their first family. Some are so bitter and regretful that they are unwilling to provide a second or third wife, even a fraction of the lifestyle given to their first wife. Yet, they expect a new partner to provide most, if not all, of the benefits received from their first wife.

Having a clear idea of what you'd like your partner's financial standing to be, which at minimum should support your current lifestyle, is a must. No woman should entertain a partner whose financial standing is so questionable that it forces her to downsize from a life she was able to maintain as a single woman. That's not only a sign of esteem issues but also a grave misunderstanding of business acumen. A romantic relationship, especially one leading to marriage, is a business decision that should not be entered on a whim or need to fill a void, especially in midlife. Having potential is expected and, to some degree, accepted of men under forty, but for men over forty, potential should be at full capacity, bearing tangible fruit of its labor. While times have changed and individual roles in relationships are ever-changing, one thing that will stand the test of time and trends is the desire to experience relationships that bring out the best in us and foster an environment of authenticity, respect, peace and reciprocal love.

Answer these questions in your next journal entry:

- How will you balance independence while being part of a relationship?

- Excluding parenting, what accomplishments are you most proud of?

- What roles have spirituality or personal beliefs played in guiding your life decisions?

- What habits or routines contribute positively to your life, and which are holding you back?

- What role does self-care play in your life, and how have you practiced it?

"Sometimes your joy is the source of your smile, but sometimes your smile can be the source of your joy."
— Thich Nhat Hanh

PART FIVE

Body Image in Midlife

Perfect Mirror Broken Soul

"Definitions belong to the defines, not the defined." —
Toni Morrison

January 13, 2015 — It Comes and Goes — San Diego, CA

Two things happen to women once they pass society's acceptable age for being thought youthful and desirable: some are bombarded with comments complimenting their ability to look young for their age, while others receive unsolicited advice on the best ways to look young and desirable for their age. As a society, we've taught women that no matter their accomplishments, contribution to society, or internal struggles, their entire existence is tied to their ability to maintain a physically desirable and youthful appearance.

Mature women are excluded, or maybe even forgotten during conversations on self-love and self-acceptance until it's time to showcase that rare unicorn who seems to be defying visible signs of aging through plastic surgery and other so-called anti-aging practices. The ability to maintain a youthful look, even when going through life-altering changes, is seen as a success, while deciding to embrace the natural aging process and look your age is frowned upon. It is as if making peace with having visible signs of aging is a sign that you've let yourself go or punishment for bad behavior.

Society has done such a number on women that many will downplay and make light of the privilege of aging— discounting the beauty and privilege of reaching milestones that can only be reached after a certain age, grieving what once was, instead of showing gratitude for what is. We cling to and romanticize our younger years, even when, for most, the years before forty were some of the most unclear, self-sabotaging, self-deprecating, people-pleasing times to experience. Yet, those years are revered as our best years, as society often places a premium on youthfulness. The belief that we are our most worthy, valuable, and desirable before signs of life appear on our face and body has shaped our who and significantly impacted our why.

JOCELYN

"I didn't rediscover myself until my mid-fifties, better late than never, right? In my twenties, I took a multitude of wrong turns and made many poor choices. In my thirties, I frantically looked for a lifeline to pull me out of an ever-deepening bleak rut that seemed to last a lifetime. In my late fifties, I had the awakening everyone talked about and began sitting more comfortably in my skin. At sixty-two, I retired, and it was then that I had consistent freedom to recall and bring to life aspirations that were put on the back burner while I navigated 'real life.' I began thinking about all the dreams and goals that used to keep me up at night in my youth before society told me I had limitations. I was what they call a tomboy growing up; I didn't care for all the frills and extra pretty things most girls think about. I've always been average-built and grew up in a family of athletes, so in my younger years, my focus was to build and maintain strength and celebrate the functions of my body instead of its ability to look sexually desirable and youthful.

But in my late forties to early fifties, somewhere between my divorce and going through the many physical and hormonal changes of menopause, I began to regress and internalize unrealistic expectations of what I should and shouldn't look like for a woman my age. Mirrors became reminders of what once was, and I began tweaking, pulling, and changing my body through plastic surgery and other cosmetic procedures. I began experiencing the multitude of insecurities and self-doubt that most women experience in puberty. It's like my body was aging and behaving as it should for a woman my age and lifestyle, but my mind was stuck in a pubescent state, questioning and disliking every single change occurring in my body. Don't get me wrong; I don't regret any of the enhancements I've made to improve my look. However, I have a very addictive personality, so one procedure led to another and another, with each improvement shedding light on brand-new flaws that I convinced myself needed fixing.

There were months when I had acne like I was a thirteen-year-old girl, and my weight fluctuated wildly despite following the same diet that's kept me healthy and slim my entire life. My body had a mind of its own, and it took me years to learn how to care for it, accept this new stage of my development, and quiet outside voices to determine what the next twenty years and beyond would look like. In retrospect, I realize I didn't always like my body or the changes occurring within, but I loved and appreciated its resilience. I think that's what's missing in this conversation. Women should feel comfortable voicing their dislike of the changes occurring in their bodies and allowed space and grace to work through days where they don't feel beautiful without it being interpreted as self-hating or someone who hates the aging process.

Several weeks ago, while having dinner with a close friend, we found ourselves going down memory lane; feeling nostalgic, I pulled out our high school yearbook. Next to my photo in the comment section under, 'Where do you see yourself twenty years from now?' I wrote, happy. While we've long passed the twenty-year mark, and it took me a long time to get here, I am, for the most part, happy. It comes and goes naturally, but I am at a place where I no longer beat up on myself on days when I wake up, and my body needs a bit more TLC to get going. Nor am I only happy when I am told I look good for my age. That kind of balance is life-changing. Time passes, and we age. Some days I look like I am on top of the world, and other days I look like the world sits heavy on my face and shoulders, and that's okay."

Jocelyn passed away on October 19, 2022, at seventy-one. I am immensely grateful to have had the opportunity to meet, break bread, and experience aging through her eyes. For that and her, I am eternally grateful.

Ageism and fatphobia are two of the most accepted forms of prejudice worldwide. Old and fat jokes are the safest and most accepted type of "funny." What would not pass the vibe test if said of other groups is comedic gold when said of older and/or fat people. It was not too long ago that the concept of body positivity, which began in the sixties, was reintroduced on social media to encourage conversations on society's inability to accept and respect bigger bodies and highlight the dangers of diet culture.

For those living in bodies marginalized by society for being fat, disabled, or other, body positivity was introduced to demand visibility and respect for all. I remember explicitly when the body-positive movement became popular on social media. It was early 2010, and creators of all shapes, sizes, imperfections, and lifestyles began using their corner of the internet to stand proudly in their skin, determined to redefine and reshape the narrative around beauty and give voice to those often pushed aside as undesirable and unworthy of love, never mind respect.

As a mother to two young adult daughters, I was delighted to witness such a movement and did my part in spreading the word far and wide. But, like all movements regarding the empowerment and upliftment of women, physical appearance remains the building block for determining worthiness and value. Beneath well-intend think pieces, catchy jargon, and youth-obsessed pictures and videos were reminders that when it comes to change and addressing issues ailing women, change is more digestible when presented in a younger, much thinner body.

And, no other body is more empowering, valuable, and worthy of existing than that of a 20-something woman. What began as a movement to humanize marginalized groups, specifically those living in bigger bodies, turned into a desire to prove that one can be beautiful and fat...at the same time. Positive self-image became synonymous with feeling and declaring 'I am beautiful,' even when you didn't feel it.

Inherent beauty was pushed to the back burner, giving a bigger platform to beauty as it relates to our shell. So, it wasn't surprising that women of a certain age were not included in such a movement. When it comes to changing the narrative and our perceptions of beauty, aging is never included in conversations surrounding uplifting and accepting the natural aging process. It is as if those who are outside the unrealistic age-specific beauty standards are no longer viable members of society and, therefore, do not need space for pep talks, empowerment, and acceptance.

In comes body neutrality. I would like to believe that social exclusion and marginalization played a significant role in bringing to life the idea of body neutrality. Body neutrality is said to be the middle ground between body positivity and body negativity. It seeks to change the narrative on unconditional self-love to include body neutrality. The term appeared online in late 2015. It grew in popularity when Anne Poirier, a certified intuitive eating counselor and eating disorder specialist, began using the phrase to help clients build a healthier balance between food and exercise. Poirier, defined body neutrality as "prioritizing the body's function, focusing on what it can do instead of its appearance."

It supports the concept that we don't have to love or hate our bodies. We can feel neutral about them without shame or need to explain those feelings. Body neutrality gives space to bodies of all sizes and ages. It examines all developmental processes and provides women the freedom to speak openly about the ups and downs of their changing bodies without feeling the need to proclaim self-love (fake it till you feel it) or feel guilty when they may love their bodies, but don't necessarily like what it's doing at a particular time or season.

Aging, with all its ups and downs, is incredibly humbling. Making peace with the fact that your physical appearance may not mirror how you feel or how you think about yourself is a challenge in and of itself. Being part of a community or movement where bodies are celebrated for their function, without judgment or expectation to present as someone no longer part of your now, is refreshing and incredibly empowering. Body neutrality is appreciating your health and what your body is capable of doing instead of focusing on or placing value on yourself for how you look. It's making peace with the fact that you won't always feel beautiful, and that's okay. It's being grateful for a body that didn't give up on you, even when you wanted to give up on it.

For women going through the many stages of perimenopause and menopause, embracing a body-neutral mindset will create the balance needed to face days when it feels like your body is working against you. A reminder to honor bodies that have supported you through all circumstances, even amidst poor choices and misconceptions of their purpose. It encourages appreciation of bones that continue to hold you up and move you forward, even when you didn't think you'd make it past your twenties. It encourages a mindset of gratefulness and focuses on embracing fine lines and scars representing all the dreams and people we've birth to life. It forces us to dig deep and ask those tough questions. Like, who taught you to define your worth based on unrealistic aging standards? As I write this chapter, I've just come back from seeing a naturopathic doctor for chronic sciatic pain due to a herniated disc. In December 2019, my health took a turn that left me with ongoing mobility and sensory issues that have changed the way I treat my body and support it through the aging process. Changes from how I speak to it and about it, to understanding the importance of paying attention to the warning signs it sends, alerting me when it's not at ease.

As I began educating myself on changes that were, in fact, associated with aging versus those that are signs of other underlying symptoms of dis-ease unrelated to aging, I began to see aging not as this evil process that comes to still my joy but as part of a process that encourages me to see my role in the demise and health of my existence. Educating myself on the physiological changes that are normal and expected parts of aging and understanding the natural processes of aging helped me recognize and appreciate the physical, mental, and emotional changes accompanying aging, which helped me fully embrace and appreciate my body's evolution.

This change in my health was the catalyst for creating strategies that are now part of my self-care routine. Whether physical or mental, healing will not happen overnight; unlearning unrealistic societal standards will require time and work. It's normal to relapse and have moments of doubt, but with consistent effort and self-compassion, you can make significant strides in improving your relationship with your body.

But you must resolve to treat yourself with the same kindness and understanding that you would offer a loved one or a friend. Be gentle with yourself and reframe negative thoughts and self-criticism that are not constructive. Ask yourself, are these thoughts based on facts or distorted perceptions, based on unhealed trauma or unrealistic societal expectations? Language shapes perceptions; be mindful of how you speak to yourself and of yourself. Be aware of self-deprecating jokes. Cultivate the use of positive language that celebrates your journey instead of perpetuating negative stereotypes. Use positive affirmations to counteract negative self-talk. Remind yourself of your strengths, accomplishments, and those things you appreciate most about your body.

Shift your focus from appearance-based goals to health and well-being goals. Engage in activities that make you feel good physically and mentally, focusing more on health and less on appearance. Concentrate on what your body can do rather than how it meets society's expectations of a body worthy of love and respect. You are more than your ability to remain f!@%-able at any age. Reduce exposure to media that promotes unrealistic beauty standards. Unfollow or mute social media accounts that evoke feelings of inadequacy or trigger negative thoughts.

Advocate for yourself and your well-being. Set boundaries with people who make negative comments about your appearance. Spend time with people who support and uplift you. Surrounding yourself with positive influences can boost your self-esteem and confidence and provide alternatives to unrealistic expectations seen in the media.

If body image issues are significantly impacting your well-being, consider seeking support from a mental health professional, such as a therapist or counselor. There is no shame in seeking help to fully grasp the changes happening in your body. Make use of your resources, and remain open to learning new ways of embracing and living in your changing body. Your willingness to seek help, even when unsure of the answers you are seeking, will help you appreciate your aging body and begin working with it and not against it. Educate yourself on unrealistic beauty standards perpetuated by society. Recognizing that aging is a natural process and beauty comes in diverse forms, is the beginning of creating a culture where women of your generation and future generations challenge social norms and age on their own terms. Cultivate a sense of gratitude for your body's resilience and the experiences it has carried you through.

Appreciating your body's functionality can shift your perspective. Understand that bodies naturally change with age, and perfection is unattainable. However, valuing your inner qualities, personality, intelligence, and kindness will contribute significantly to overall attractiveness and well-being. Keep a journal where you write down things you're grateful for, including positive aspects of your body and achievements. Embracing the natural aging process is not merely about acknowledging the passage of time; it is about cultivating a mindset that celebrates the wisdom and experiences that come with each passing year, ultimately enriching the quality of life now and many years to come.

Answer these questions in your next journal entry:

- Finish this sentence: life is _____.

- In what way will you embrace and appreciate the aging process rather than fear it?

- What does body positivity or body neutrality look like in your life?

- What does joy look like in your life?

- When it comes to _____, I am my own worst enemy.

"Courage doesn't always roar. Sometimes, courage is the quiet voice at the end of the day saying, 'I will try again tomorrow.'" — Mary Anne Radmacher

Anti-aging is Anti-life

We are the ones we've been waiting for." — June Jordan

January 13, 2015 — Turn Back Time — San Diego, California

As our children prepare to start their journey into adulthood, we, too, begin to sit a bit more fully into a journey that many would prefer to skip. One day, you're a hip and happening new mom; you blink for a second and find yourself standing in front of a mirror to an older, perhaps wiser stranger looking back at you, challenging your hip and happeningness. The opportunity to experience the physical changes associated with aging is an invaluable gift, yet it can also be incredibly humbling. To live long enough to have visible signs of your life story meticulously and softly etched into the corners of your mouth is a reminder of days when boisterous laughter, immeasurable joy, and mischief envelop every corner of your home. Where sounds of command, exasperated breaths, and laughter, hung in the air like a fresh batch of pancakes, smothered in warm maple syrup, topped with slightly sweet caramel-flavored butter. Where commands like, "Wake up! Go to sleep! Pick that up!" And, "One day, you'll miss my nagging!" are said as often as whispers of unconditional love and pride— "I love you to the moon and back! You are my wildest dreams realized! For this child, I prayed!" Where years of strategizing and planning now sit between fading eyebrows as reminders of days when "living on a prayer" was not only your favorite song but a wayward string, holding the last bit of hope when what you now call life was but a dream.

I'd like to believe that much of our resistance to aging is not as superficial as society would like us to believe. Making peace with the person staring back at you in the mirror goes beyond cremes, oils, and expensive treatments. And it's not as simple as just accepting aging as a natural part of life. It requires self-compassion, audacity, and freedom to fully explore ways to connect who you are now with the person you're becoming. It's an understanding that while you may not feel like how you look, how you look shouldn't determine your potential or your worth.

Fear of aging is neither above nor beneath any of us. It is not isolated to a particular group and is not a sign of self-hate or low esteem. Fear of aging, or rather, fear that we are in a period where we are closer to our sunset than we are to our sunrise, is quite the awakening. One of the most painful reminders contributing to our resistance to aging is the realization that we may one day reach an age where there is more to look back at than to look forward to. The concept of trying to delay or reverse the effects of aging is not new and has been around in various forms throughout history. Humans have always sought ways to maintain their youthfulness and vitality.

Our interpretation of what aging is and is not is strongly tied to societal influences, cultural norms, personal experiences, media representation, financial standing, and individual mindset. Our perception of self and how we should or shouldn't age is strongly connected to parameters that measure our worth, not based on our contributions to society or lived experiences, but on how graceful or ungraceful we appear to be aging.

Idioms such as aging gracefully are used to bind and put us in a box. Where the memory of who we were and past experiences represent the all of us. Where new dreams, new experiences, and creativity go to die. Aging gracefully is to adults what "children should be seen and not heard" is to young children. You're allowed to exist but do so quietly, with very little fuss or discourse of its challenges. Aging gracefully is conditional; it says you are only as graceful as your willingness to not shake the table or challenge the status quo. Grace, in relation to age, is a concept devoid of empathy, ingenuity, and grace itself. You can age, but try your best not to look it.

You can age, but do so quietly. Aging gracefully is where creativity goes to die.

Two time periods have significantly shaped society's view of aging and its potential to make or break us. From the 16th to the 18th century, the focus was on extending individual lives and prioritizing the vitality of older adults; scholars and practitioners of care alike believed aging was a time of considerable value and people age at different rates due to various genetic, environmental, and lifestyle factors. Therefore, using chronological age as the sole measure ignores the wide range of biological variability in how individuals age. And, since biological aging occurs at the cellular level, chronological age theory does an incomplete job of capturing the cellular dimension of aging. However, by the twentieth century, two changes occurred, both reshaping society's concept of aging and youthfulness. Aging was, in fact, measured chronologically, which defined old age as starting at 65, and the term "anti-aging," as we know it today, grew with the rise of the beauty and cosmetic industry.

Advances in medical technology, cosmetic surgery, and skincare products led to the marketing of various treatments and products under the label "anti-aging." Miracle cremes, oils, and treatments became cover to hide an insidious dislike of aging and older people.

While some of these approaches have demonstrated effectiveness in improving skin appearance, which in and of itself is not necessarily bad, the term "anti-aging" itself is not only controversial but an oxymoron. Anti-aging rhetoric implies aging is inherently negative; it robs us of our beauty and youthful vitality. It ushers in the start of cellular decline and decreases, if not completely erases, our desirability factor; therefore, it should be fought, if not eradicated, by any means necessary. From a purely superficial standpoint, supporting or believing the claims of anti-aging supporters wouldn't be so bad if the primary goal was to market cremes and oils that improve overall skin appearance and "reduce" fine lines. However, that is not the case. This idea goes beyond wrinkle creme and face mask. There is a blatant hate of aging, which transfers into the dismissal and invisibility of older adults (primarily women), that is both unnerving and incredibly dangerous. Three mindsets develop when we measure aging solely from the standpoint of numbers on our birth certificate and how those numbers affect our who and why:

- One, we live by an "it is what it is" mindset, where we believe there is not much we can do about what is said to be the negative parts of aging. We leave its progression and how it manifests in our body to luck, removing ourselves as pilots of what drives it to what we call its "bad state." We live in a state of panic and anxiety, stagnantly awaiting a decline that may or may not happen.

- Secondly, we measure the aging process by its presentation on the exterior. We lament over fine lines, wrinkles, and gray hair, completely discounting the functions of the body that are, in fact, working quite well. We stay in a perpetual state of doubting our capabilities due to societal beliefs of what a person of a certain age can and can't do. We focus on appearing young, while internally, we are aging long before "old age" sets in. We ask, what will I look like as I continue on this journey? Instead of, how do I change my behavior to increase my chances for longevity and flourish and thrive in my aging body?

- Thirdly, we make light, if not completely dismiss, our accomplishments and contributions to our family and society. We buy into the belief that we're now useless, with very little to offer and even less time for new experiences, as our best days are behind us. We feed into stereotypes and assumptions that rob us of our individuality and creativity, thereby positioning ourselves to a one-dimensional existence.

Sandy

"I turned sixty last month and went into full panic mode. It's like the clock struck twelve, forcing a switch to turn on in my mind, alerting me that the countdown has begun. Growing up, my parents had a poster near the medicine cabinet in their bathroom that read, 'Today is the first day of the rest of your life.' I hated that poster. I took it down every chance I got and hid it, but my mother always found it and would hang it right back up as if it were part of a to-do list. Not sure if she saw it as a reminder to seize the day or a reminder of how unfair life is when it comes to life and death, but it stayed on that wall for the entirety of my middle school years until we moved to another house, and thankfully, was lost in the shuffle.

I've been thinking a lot about that poster, as I am at the age where time is not on my side, something said frequently by the older women in my community growing up. There was so much negativity around aging that even though I hoped to live a long life, the fear associated with the potential breakdown of the body that happens as you age weighed heavily on my heart. I'm not too worried about visible signs of aging on my face or body; I didn't start getting work done until my late forties. Like most women in my family, we don't start showing visible signs of aging until well into our mid to late sixties, but if you can name a chronic illness associated with aging, we have them all. As my daughters would say, 'the face card never declines,' but the body, the body does, and that is my biggest fear with aging. What will become of me and my body as I age." **writes Sandy**

Aging is often presented as a disease, with those starting the process frantically searching for remedies and methods to stop its progression as its progression is like steps leading to illnesses and diseases that question the supposed "blessing" aspect of aging. If your only source of reference regarding women and their feelings on aging are articles and data compiled by the beauty industry, you'd think most women hate aging or are afraid of aging from a purely superficial perspective. While skin care treatments are among the most purchased items by women between the ages of twenty-five and fifty, if you were to poll women on the reasons for their purchase and desire to maintain a youthful appearance, the responses go beyond women simply wanting to look and be twenty-five again. The search for the fountain of youth is not simply to look like their past selves but to control and repair externally, what many women believe to be out of their control internally.

I have, and I'm sure you've met people who appear much older than their chronological age, who, due to life choices, genetics, social and financial standing, and misunderstandings of what aging is and is not, are impacted by disease one would consider, an older person's disease. While another person might be chronologically older yet still have a high level of physical and cognitive function, due to genetics, and healthy and positive aging practices. To believe that illness and old age are inextricably intertwined or synonymous is to buy into the rhetoric that aging is all bad, something to dread and seek to destroy.

Changing the conversation to answer what aging is and what it's not objectively is the first step to freeing our minds of anti-aging rhetoric. When we stop viewing age, or getting older, as an enemy to be eradicated, we position ourselves in a place where we live and thrive in the richness and rewards of aging. We lean into the wealth of knowledge, wisdom, life experiences, and problem-solving skills that are the cornerstone of our existence to determine best practices for aging on our terms, devoid of fear-mongering antics and remorse for what once was.

Miranda

I am what my mother would call someone who bloomed much later in life. As a teenager, while most of my relatives and peers looked like they came out of the womb in full bloom, I was the complete opposite; my beauty needed time to cook and settle. Growing up, I wasn't seen as the pretty one; my mother would tease me, saying I looked like my father's people. You wouldn't know this or even believe this if you met me now, as I believe I've shrunk considerably since my teenage years, but I was, in my youth, an awkwardly tall and lanky girl with very pronounced features and a voice way too deep for a young girl. You see, back when I was growing up, there was not much diversity in beauty. No matter your race or ethnicity, smaller, less pronounced features were the epitome of beauty. These beauty standards were not only present in the multitude of billboards, magazines, and television shows shoved in our faces, but they were the standards adopted by many of the women in my family. My teenage years through my late twenties were beyond challenging.

Although much of what she said was said in jest, my mother's teasing would sit at the back of my mind when thinking about dating and overall view of myself and what I will look like as I age. We have a saying in my family that you can't be a double negative, which meant I couldn't be unattractive and dumb, so I worked hard to always be at the top of my classes. For many women in my family and in my immediate circle, their face was their passport, the key that opened doors that most wouldn't even know existed, nonetheless have access to. It was drilled in me from a young age that I did not have such privilege. So I focused on intelligence, and by the time my features caught up with the global initiative to embrace all beauty types, the opinions of others no longer mattered to me, and I became the rich man my mother said I couldn't pull. It took a while to love my less-than-conventional features; by a while, I mean almost fifty years. The older I got, the more my features continued to settle and "fit" my face, with other body parts, like my hips and thighs, following suit, and I began to look proportional for my age, height, and stature.

At fifty-nine, I am so comfortable in my skin that the thought of being twenty, or even thirty again, is an absolute no; thank you! This is the best I've looked and felt my entire life. Not to mention, I am slowly entering the season where I am invisible to the male gaze, which adds an extra pep to my steps. Any health or wellness initiative taken on my part is done to support my peace of mind and internal joy. I wouldn't turn back time even if I could. I've worked extremely hard at repairing the damage I did to myself due to parental and societal pressure to fit into an unrealistic beauty box and attempt to slow down visible signs of aging. No longer do I consider society's unrealistic beauty standards as gospel, nor do I subscribe to the idea that aging is a death sentence to be rushed through. Because the opposite of aging is a place I am not ready to visit. – **Miranda**

While the perception of beauty is highly subjective and can vary widely from person to person, we've been sold a lie that we are only as beautiful as our ability to fit into society's very specific and narrow beauty standards and body trends of the day. Trends that are usually dependent on our ability to appear youthful, F-able, and ageless. Physical features and capabilities change as we age; accepting that fact and creating individual standards that go beyond wanting to be twenty-five again position us in a place where we can stand proudly and confidently on the belief that, youthful features and youthful presentation, do not solely define what beauty is and is not. Challenging stereotypes that perpetuate a linear beauty standard and recognizing that beauty is not solely dependent on age or physical appearance is the mindset shift needed when attempting to reshape the conversation. A shift that can potentially change society's perceptions of beauty as it relates to youth, aging, and extending one's lifespan.

While extending lifespan is a common goal in anti-aging research, the focus should ideally be on improving health span – the period of life spent in good health – rather than merely prolonging life. Attempting to prolong life without addressing the quality of life during those extra years is like winning the lottery, while having little to no understanding of the role of money in our lives; both, if not handled properly, can cause more harm than good. How beneficial is desiring to live a long life if those years are lived in longer periods of frailty and dependency?

I would be remiss not to acknowledge the many challenges associated with aging. From ageism in the workplace to the horror that is dating after age fifty, to the ups and downs of menopause, to coping with the rollercoaster of emotions that comes with life as an empty nester, aging is not linear. Still, the conversation should not lead with how best to stop its progression or eradicate it completely. But more so, how do we change the current life model to one where aging individuals are taught early how to prepare for those changes. And work to create a society that actively practice inclusivity beyond catchy phrases and hashtags. We must shift our attention and actively cultivate innovative ideas and approaches that stimulate change beyond the limitations of outdated thinking and practices.

When we speak of aging or getting older as something to eradicate, we are telling those within that group that they are no longer valuable, that their time is up, with nothing to look forward to or offer society. The quest to eradicate the aging process is both dehumanizing and incredibly dismissive. It supports an ideology that promotes the maltreatment of older people. It contributes to the marginalization of older individuals, and perpetuates harmful stereotypes. It focuses on increasing longevity without much thought on one's quality of life.

In the early stages of our youth, we are often asked, "What do you want to be when you grow up?" A question that becomes a significant part of our who and why. Whether we can answer that question in our youth or later in life, our answer, if not examined with an open mind, can force us into careers and life experiences that stifle our creativity and self-expression. Where glass ceilings keep us in a perpetual state of should-haves and could-haves. Whether you've already lived your wildest dreams in your youth or are still trying to figure it out, aging is your blank card. When we embrace aging and make peace with its progression, we can answer and bring to life the question of who instead of what. Who do you want to be now, in this new season of your life? Making peace with the aging process and embracing the many ups and downs associated with this journey provides the opportunity to add life to your days and worry less about how many days are left in your life.

The only remedy to combat aging is to view it not as something to remedy, but as an opportunity to create your own narrative of vitality and fulfillment. But you must resolve to be a present and active participant in the ups and downs of your life. You must be open to all opportunities for learning and growth. Nurturing a mindset that time, no matter how fast it appears to be moving, is not your enemy. When used wisely, time can serve as a conduit for joy, peace, and transformational opportunities.

Answer these questions in your next journal entry:

- When do you feel most fulfilled or alive?

- What do you tend to procrastinate on, and why?

- How do you challenge traditional notions of aging?

- How do you feel your perceptions of aging have evolved as you've transitioned into midlife?

"I understood that I was inventing myself, and that I was doing this more in the way of a painter than in the way of a scientist. I could not count on precision or calculation; I could only count on intuition." — Jamaica Kincaid

PART SIX
Family Affair

Caring for Aging Parents

"Love is like the rain. It comes in a drizzle sometimes. Then it starts pouring and if you're not careful it will drown you." — Edwidge Danticat

September 19, 2016 — A Commandment & A Promise — Long Is. City, NY

"How apt that he would die first, leaving me to care for his wife, so on brand of him," said Cami as she cut into the Margherita pizza we ordered. We are sitting outside Tappo's in Chelsea, NYC. It is the third week of September, and while it's starting to get cooler, the warm sun hitting my face and chest feels like the beginning of Indian Summer. "I knew this day would come and knew no matter where I was when it happened, a trip back home was a must. But I never thought about or planned for what my role would be if he died first. You know Mama's always been sickly. Our biggest fear growing up was that we would one day come home to her lying dead on the living room floor or admitted to the hospital and never return. I never thought about the possibility of him going first. I don't want to be known as the person who abandoned her mother during her most difficult time, you know what I mean?"

It was a rhetorical question, but I knew exactly what she meant. Cami and I share a similar upbringing; we were both groomed to be little women before fully understanding how to be little girls. We met in high school, in 4th period English Lit class; she was the girl everyone wanted to befriend. A biracial girl with deep caramel skin and prominent features that made it easy for her to identify as fully Black. She had deep brown eyes that appeared hazel when kissed by the sun and long, unruly hair that was just as stubborn as she is. She wore multi-colored glasses that covered deep brown freckles that looked like stardust left behind by a passing comet, adding a touch of whimsy to her appearance. Mix-match socks were her signature look, and in Winter, she wore leg warmers that matched her colorful hairbands and scrunchies; she looked like a real-life teenage Punky Brewster (one of the cutest TV shows of the 80s).

"I am not saying I wanted her to go first; that's not what I'm saying at all," she continued, looking directly at me as if to make sure I didn't misinterpret her feelings. "You remember how she treated me; she was downright cruel. Even now, at forty-two, she continues to see me and speak to me as if I am a sixteen-year-old girl with no direction, correction, a 'fast' sixteen-year-old girl with no direction— that was her favorite way to describe me, remember? How do I fulfill my duties and honor her as my mother, doing what's expected of me while still having so many questions and resentment over her treatment of me?"

We grew up in very similar homes. While my father "died" when I was twelve, which left my mother to raise me and my siblings alone, her father, who was a long-distance truck driver, was away more than he was home. Leaving her to navigate life with an angry and resentful mother, who, on the one hand, would brag and exotify her biracial children in public yet would not let a day go by without reminding Cami that she was the darkest of her two siblings and should act accordingly.

"No one is coming to save you," she would say, her gaze moving from Cami to me. "Focus on your books and studies; that's all you have. Don't follow Kelsey's crazy ways; you two don't have what she has." For a long time, I didn't understand her mother's warning and couldn't for the life of me put my finger on what she believed was lacking in us that put us in the category of people unworthy of saving, especially since Cami was her literal twin.

Cami has two siblings; she and her oldest sister, Kelsey, are three years apart, with her brother Christopher, following immediately after her birth; Irish twins, they called them, as they were only fourteen or so months apart. Her sister was a well-carved copy of their paternal grandmother, having honey-blond hair that cascaded down her back in loose waves, deep green eyes, and a scattering of freckles adoring her cheeks and brows. She was much thinner than Cami and 'lucky' not to be full-figured, with what their mother called child-bearing hips.

Even though she was the oldest of the three children, she was shown immense grace and relieved of many responsibilities usually set apart for the oldest child. They say parents don't or, rather, shouldn't have favorites when it comes to their children, but if you asked Cami, she would say her mother didn't get that memo. Our mothers, although not related, were cut from the same cloth. One that envelopes the idea that children are at the center of their parents' retirement plans. Therefore, are groomed from an early age to show unconditional gratitude and loyalty to their parents just on the basis of them being their parents and raising them as best they could— no matter how shabby of a job they've done.

Caring for aging parents is a challenging and often emotionally charged responsibility. Caring for elderly parents who were once abusive requires confronting a painful and tumultuous past that can evoke a wide range of emotions— anger, resentment, and fear. Unhealed wounds from past abuse can resurface, making it difficult to provide compassionate care without becoming overwhelmed by negative feelings. It can be challenging to reconcile feelings of empathy and compassion with memories of abuse, creating an emotional rollercoaster.

One of the most significant challenges associated with being caregivers to formerly abusive parents is striking a balance between compassion for our parents' needs while protecting ourselves from potential harm. There's often a fear that revisiting the past might lead to retraumatization, making self-protection essential. It's not uncommon for children who find themselves as caretakers to abusive parents to struggle with feelings of guilt and shame. Guilt often stems from questioning whether they owe their abusive parents care and support. Shame can arise from societal judgment or feeling responsible for the abuse suffered as children. Overcoming these emotions is critical when attempting to provide adequate care without compromising mental and emotional well-being.

For children raised in homes where much was expected of them with no consideration of their needs and feelings, understanding and creating boundaries that protect and center them as the important person in the story can be incredibly challenging. This manifests greatly when put in positions where they must consider their needs and wellbeing over those of a loved one, even when the loved one has caused them harm. And it's especially challenging when that loved one is a parent.

"And you know she played the religious card, right? Telling me God will honor and repay me for honoring and caring for her in her time of need. Where was this God when she was beating me black and blue and shaming me in front of her church friends? And why hasn't this God repay her for her treatment of me?" She asked, but I knew not to respond, as we both knew the answer.

Cami paused, took a sip of red wine, and turned to look at the sidewalk where a crowd had begun to grow. She began touching her hair, which made me realize the depth of her pain and resentment for being put in the position of caretaker to her mom. When we were teenagers, whenever her mom was around, she would pull at the front of her hair to a point where it was almost painful to watch. Watching her manipulate her hair now felt like we were teenagers again, but only this time, the decision to be loving or a complete monster was in our hands.

"It never fails," she continued, "each time I think I've moved on and I am no longer affected by what she thinks of me or how she treated me, something like this happens, forcing me to revisit her and that time in my life. I think I've healed; you know I have, and you and I both know she hasn't. Her playing nice is just an old woman trying to get to heaven while dragging me through hell."

I knew exactly what Cami meant and felt anxious just thinking about what awaited her. As someone who grew up in a religious household, where the lines between discipline and child abuse were blurred, if not completely nonexistent, God was the excuse used for all maltreatment of those who should be seen and not heard. Fear of God was strategically drilled into us to ensure when we no longer fear our parents, our fear of God would serve as a moral compass, encouraging us to remain loyal to our parents and expectations that may not be to our benefit. If you didn't know any better, you'd think God is more on the side of the abuser than the abusee. God, as presented to us children, was harsh, cold, and cruel, offering very little room for mistakes, nonetheless, redemption. Which was represented in the way many parents of the church treated their children, especially the oldest. They behaved like the God they presented to us, holding us to unrealistic standards, all while withholding those tools needed to live up to those standards.

Establishing and maintaining boundaries is crucial when caring for formerly abusive parents. To people raised in abusive environments, boundaries are not only a foreign concept, but feel disloyal to their parents. To establish boundaries is to go against the concept of unconditional loyalty and respect expected in a toxic child/parent relationship. Unlearning such a concept is no easy feat. It requires a solid understanding of what boundaries are and what they should look like in the parent/child relationship, as well as an understanding of how to set them all while remaining true to yourself and your core values.

Setting healthy boundaries will differ from person to person. For example, while I may have the capacity to frequently engage and personally care for my parents and still maintain boundaries by knowing when to leave and when to stay (prioritizing self-care in the form of seeking respite care, taking breaks and maintaining my own physical and emotional wellbeing), another person may decide to hire a caretaker to avoid direct daily contact. Neither one is good or bad, and there is no shame in choosing the option that may not be ideal for your parents, but protects your mental, emotional, and physical well-being.

The same rule applies to forgiveness. Forgiveness is a complex and deeply personal process for caregivers of formerly abusive parents. Some may choose to forgive, while others may not. There are those who choose not to forgive and develop feelings of indifference, where a parent's behavior is not seen as something to correct or accept but just is what it is. Indifference can serve as a shield against negativity or toxic behavior. It can help in maintaining your inner peace by not allowing someone else's behavior to affect your mental or emotional state.

And for those who choose to forgive, forgiveness does not mean forgetting or condoning past abuse but a step toward personal healing and closure. Yet still, while forgiveness and reconciliation may be goals for some, it is essential to recognize that they are not obligatory. The caregiving journey is deeply personal, and each person must make choices that align with their values and emotional well-being. Setting boundaries and having a clear understanding of your limits is crucial in all types of relationships, not just in toxic ones, as they serve as cornerstone for healthy interactions, mutual respect, and emotional well-being.

Establishing boundaries enables you to maintain well-being, ensuring you have the energy and emotional resilience to provide the best care possible. It involves recognizing the importance of self-care, which can look like, setting aside time for personal activities, and seeking support when needed. By nurturing your own well-being, you increase your chances to better support aging parents without compromising your own health. The responsibilities of caregiving can be overwhelming, often leading to caregiver burnout— a state of physical, emotional, and mental exhaustion. Knowing one's limits and setting boundaries is essential to prevent burnout. This includes understanding the level of care one can provide without sacrificing your own health or quality of life. Learning to say "no" when necessary, seeking assistance from other members of the family, support groups or professional caregivers, and setting realistic expectations are crucial strategies, when trying to avoid burnout. Recognizing limits doesn't signify failure, but rather a proactive approach that ensures sustainable and quality care for your parents, and support for your own well-being.

Answer these questions in your next journal entry:

- How do you distinguish healthy caution versus paralyzing fear in decision-making?

- Finish this sentence, one way I prioritize myself is by _____.

- You are back in your childhood home; who's with you and what are you doing?

- How was your childhood different from that of your children?

- I can compromise on most things except_____.

"And the day came when the risk to remain tight in a bud was more painful than the risk it took to blossom."— Anais Nin

Relationship With Adult Children

"If only there could be an invention that bottled up a memory, like scent. And it never faded, and it never got stale. And then, when one wanted it, the bottle could be uncorked, and it would be like living the moment all over again." —*Daphne du Maurier*

May 18, 2019 — Left Behind — San Francisco, California

No conversation about finding joy after drop-off would be complete without including the importance of having a healthy relationship with your young adult child and curating a legacy that will guide future generations. Parenting does not stop after drop-off and should not be the end of the parent-child relationship, but it takes work. Do you remember the days when you would tell your children, "I am not your friend!" and would place great emphasis on friend, to ensure they understood that a very thick line exists between your parental responsibilities and who you would be if you were their friend?

The parent-child relationship is complex. It's an evolving dynamic that changes as children grow into adulthood. It is part of the legacy we leave behind. Building and maintaining a strong relationship with adult children is a delicate balance of respect, open communication, and understanding.

It does not happen by chance or overnight, especially if the parent-child relationship was somewhat challenging in the teenage years. Knowing how and when to expand your role to be seen as a friend is essential to the parent/child relationship. For parents with more than one child, how you approach and balance the transition from parent to friend with one child may not be practical or wise to do with another. You must consider individual personality and needs, to ensure your approach doesn't cause more harm to the relationship than good.

When trying to build a healthy friendship with your children, it's incredibly important to approach each child as an individual, speaking to their individual wants and needs. Blanket parenting is never a good idea, as it may cause more harm than good. And while you may be able to have a close friendship with one child at an early age, another (second child*) may need you to remain strictly parent for a while longer before seeing you as a friend. No two children are alike; some come to teach us patience and unconditional love, while others test our willingness to stay out of jail (I kid, I kid!).

Can you see us? she texted. We arrived fifteen minutes before the start time. We took the closest seats we could find. The stadium is one of the largest in San Francisco. The seating tiers ascend in multiple levels, providing unobstructed views of the event from virtually every angle. It was noted that her graduating class was the largest of its kind and the first to graduate post-pandemic.

I stood up and looked in the direction of rows reserved for those in various STEM (Science, Technology, Engineering, and Math) programs. She and three of her closest friends could be seen waving and mouthing, "Hello, is anybody out there? Come about!" A saying from the movie Titanic that we often say when looking for each other in a crowd. I waved back and snapped a picture of her and her besties. While I felt great pride and eagerly awaited seeing them close this chapter of their lives, I couldn't help but wish they had it a little easier. They belong to a generation of young people facing unimaginable disruptions, along with political and financial instabilities. Despite these challenges, they move with remarkable power and self-assurance. One can't help but hope to live long enough to witness and be part of the changes promised by their resilience and determination to redefine what it means to be young, beautiful, and carefree.

When my daughter left for university, she left with guidance and life jewels that I hoped would help her better navigate life as a teen in the beginning stages of a chapter filled with opportunities, challenges, and self-discovery. Weeks after her return home, it became obvious that she had grown in ways that required me to not only adjust my expectations of our relationship but also remain open to reassessing my role to ensure I didn't become part of the many challenges experienced by young adults learning to define their why.

As parents, in a world that asks so much of our youth, where resources continue to decline while expectations are at an all-time high, it is so important that we don't become part of the problem or another hurdle for them to work through. Showing grace, compassion, and understanding of the times, as well as knowing how to read the room, is a vital part of the parent/young adult child relationship.

Parenting young adult children is complex. For those who don't have or didn't have healthy relationships with their own parents, or feel resentment for years lost during childrearing, nurturing a relationship where acceptance, compassion, and grace are the foundation of the relationship can feel like an incredible impossibility.

While there is no one way to cultivate and maintain healthy relationships with young adult children, having the understanding that the process starts with parents who are unafraid of looking inward when dealing with what they deem unacceptable behavior and life choices, is the first step in nurturing relationships where grace and compassion are integral parts of the process. It is extremely important to establish an environment where young adult children feel comfortable expressing their thoughts, concerns, and dreams. Regular conversations that go beyond superficial pleasantries and safe topics will help bridge generational gaps and cultivate mutual respect and understanding. It is not uncommon to hear young people talk about jealous tendencies or experiences they've endured at the hands of a parent who is jealous of their youth, carefree personalities, or life-changing opportunities (both professional and romantic) as they get older.

For parents raised in homes where they were put in a box, denied freedom of self-expression and carefree lifestyle, seeing their children explore aspirations they once had but couldn't pursue, or witnessing their child chase dreams or opportunities that were out of their reach, can trigger a sense of longing or regret, leading to feelings of jealousy. Confronting past pain and regrets as you support your adult child through the tumultuous journey of young adulthood is the first step towards nurturing a relationship free from jealousy and regret. Understanding where you are pulling from when trying to guide and advise adult children, asking yourself, is this advice coming from positive life experiences? Do I have their best interest at heart? Am I projecting or pulling from a place of regret, fear, or lack? That kind of self-reflection will ensure your advice and guidance are not coming from a place of envy or regret, but advice that will lead to a deeper connection built on empathy, mutual respect, and unconditional love.

Encouraging personal growth and finding fulfillment in one's own life outside the parent-child relationship is essential. Engaging in hobbies, pursuing interests, or seeking personal development can bring a sense of purpose and fulfillment that will lessen, if not completely decrease, feelings of jealousy and lost time. Respecting boundaries and acknowledging autonomy are essential for fostering a strong relationship. This means refraining from unsolicited advice or interference in their life choices. Recognizing their right to make decisions, even if they differ from your views, demonstrates a deep level of respect. It's crucial to remember that while the parent-child bond remains, the dynamic is now a relationship between two adults.

No relationship is immune to disagreements or misunderstandings. Nothing says I respect you as a person and my child than recognizing when an apology is needed. Offering it sincerely can mend wounds, reinforce the bond, and create an environment where adult children feel heard and respected. Similarly, the ability to forgive and move forward is essential to nurturing a strong relationship. Holding onto grudges creates distance, while forgiveness promotes healing and growth.

Good relationships are part of the legacy we leave behind and will serve as a blueprint for future generations. Legacy goes beyond material possessions; it's about the values, lessons, and positive impact we impart on our children, which can benefit future generations. It can inspire and guide children and grandchildren, showing them the values, principles, and behaviors that can lead to success and fulfillment.

Years ago, while vacationing in Stockholm, Sweden, I visited a local bookstore where I learned about Swedish Death Cleaning, known as "döstädning" in Swedish. The idea was popularized by Margareta Magnusson, a Swedish artist and author whose book titled "The Gentle Art of Swedish Death Cleaning: How to Free Yourself and Your Family from a Lifetime of Clutter" is a combination of personal anecdotes, practical advice, and

Swedish cultural insights, written to guide readers through the tedious process of decluttering, organizing possessions, and contemplating one's legacy. Her approach to Swedish Death Cleaning emphasizes the importance of taking control of one's belongings, simplifying life, and preparing for the inevitable parts of aging and mortality. While the idea of confronting one's mortality can be uncomfortable, unsettling, and morbid, this concept is not limited to a specific age or stage of life.

It is a thoughtful and realistic concept that highlights the importance of lightening the emotional burden on our loved ones, when we are no longer here to guide them on how best to handle our affairs— whether that is three months from now or thirty years from now. It's not merely about purging possessions or dwelling on the end. It's a mindful practice that encourages parents to focus on what truly matters and facilitates an organized, less burdensome transition when we're gone. It is understandable that this concept may evoke discomfort, reluctance, or total resistance. Addressing mortality and the process of preparing for one's passing can be unsettling. As Parents, we are dedicated to nurturing and protecting our children. The thought of actively preparing for our inevitable end, especially if we're relatively healthy, may evoke feelings of anxiety and fear.

But no matter your health status, this conversation is especially important if you're a single empty nester living alone, live in a different city, or an entirely different country. Life is incredibly unpredictable. Such preparation is an extension of your love, helping to reduce the emotional burden on your children and encourage conversations that transcend discomfort. It can mean ensuring your children know that if anything were to happen to you, your beloved cat Fifi and Oscar the bird get everything (we must keep them on their toes and acting right!).

For nesters living alone, such preparation can look like ensuring your kids have a spare key or know how to enter your home in case of emergencies. It can mean sharing location of important papers and how to access them. If you live in an apartment complex, what are the rules for entry in case of emergency? It's answering the question, if push comes to shove, will your children be armed with enough information to make informed decisions based on your needs and wishes?

Parenting doesn't end after drop-off; it is our responsibility as parents to ensure that our children, no matter their age, life choices, or belief system, know, whether near or far, there is one person cheering for them, praying for them, and rooting for their success in love, health, and everything in between. Such thought process does not discount the challenges associated with being a parent, as there are times when you will do all of the above, and the relationship will still go left; but that should not stop us from trying, even if we have to try from afar.

Drop-off or your children moving out is very similar to childbirth in that, no matter how many times you've done it or how many children you have, each child's experience is unique to that child and your relationship with them. If you're a parent to multiple children, you understand that no two children are alike, and your relationship with one can be very different from the other(s). I'm not talking about toxic favoritism, but having relationships with your children as individuals, not a pack. Catering to individual needs instead of group punishment, expectations, and interactions. When you have more than one child or grew up in a home with multiple siblings, you learn early that parenting is not one size fits all. What works for one may not work for others; shared DNA does not equate to shared values, expectations, or emotional and spiritual needs. The foundation of the how and why of your parenting style remains general, but individual needs will dictate approach, tone, and delivery.

My youngest daughter is my "I'm going to take the world by storm" kind of girl, while my oldest is "let's pace ourselves and enjoy the ride." I've learned their love language, needs, likes, and dislikes, so I pour into them according to their needs and refrain from letting fear and feelings of loss, dressed as concern, prevent them from reaching their full potential.

While speaking positivity, health, and success into their lives, I made sure to go over "the talk," reiterating the obvious with significant emphasis on the not-so-obvious. You know the talk, the **Six Dos for Staying Safe When Living Alone or on College Campus; see, listen, speak, do, go, and stay.**

1. If you see or feel something is off, go with your gut. Your intuition heightens when you're away from those most protective of you; listen to your gut. It is your guide, there to help you build and strengthen discernment skills.
2. Don't jump to conclusions; always ask what you want to know, never assume. Listen to learn and understand so your decisions can come from a place of clarity, where you will see things and people for who and what they are, not as you'd like them to be.
3. Speak up with your chest. You are allowed, encouraged, and expected to have a voice and to use that voice to share what is acceptable and unacceptable ways of treating you. You must establish the most visible lines that separate negotiable behaviors and expectations versus those that are a "hard pass." It's okay to have a different opinion on which state has the best

pizza (NYC) and who, dead or alive, is the greatest entertainer of all time, but your health, self-care, and safety are not up for debate. If you are ever put in a position where you must choose between your values and going with the crowd, the best option is always the former, never the latter.

4. Do have a blast. These may be your most carefree years yet. It's okay to think outside the box, try new ideas, explore and challenge new ways of thinking, but never forget why you're there.

5. Find your tribe, vet them well, and go where your unique qualities are celebrated and appreciated. You are not for everyone, and everyone is not going to be for you, and that's okay.

6. Stay focused on your individual life course, keeping your eyes on your paper. You don't have to have it all together, know it all, or have the answer for what your life will look like ten years from now. Stay in the now, tackling each course, event, and goal in the present.

As I write this chapter, two frames, each with a picture of my daughter's first day of kindergarten, are in front of me. While much has changed since they sat for the famous kindergarten picture, my wish for them remains the same—a sentiment that I know may speak to your own wish for your children.

May you never let the ups and downs of life harden you or convince you to dim your light. May you never let the doom and gloom of growing up paralyze you or keep you from pursuing your dreams.

May you seize every moment and remain present in your life story, expecting goodness to follow you wherever you go and grow. In a world determined to make your mistakes the all of you, remember to always show yourself grace and explore the freedom and gift of starting over.

If you're like me, feeling nostalgic and wondering where the time went, I encourage you to speak these truths when thinking of your not-so-little human.

I am blessed to have had the honor and privilege of raising a human, from crib to _____. I enter this new season with calm confidence, knowing that this is the beginning of my most fruitful season. My children will sow seeds of compassion and positivity that will bloom into blessings, both for themselves and their wider community. Through the guidance and values instilled in their formative years, they will grow to embody the principles of empathy, generosity, and integrity.

As they navigate life's journey, they carry within them the seeds of goodness, seeking opportunities to make a meaningful impact. Their actions, be it through acts of kindness, advocacy for justice, or dedication to service, serve as catalysts for positive change within their immediate circles and resonate outwardly, enriching the lives of those around them and fostering a community woven together by compassion and goodwill.

I have done my best; my children are my wildest dreams realized. I rise to the challenge of new beginnings; I will remain flexible and prepared to go with the flow and not against it. I cherish and appreciate what was and feel blessed to be entering my most transformative season, yet.

There is no greater joy and privilege than seeing your children put into practice those sayings and guidance that you thought were going to deaf ears. Trust me when I say, they were listening. They are going to be okay, and you, too, will be okay. As you begin this next phase, I encourage you to keep a journal of this new season. Relax your shoulders, close your eyes, and take a deep breath; you've done a fantastic job, mama! Trust the process and remain open to all possibilities.

I wish you a life where you experience those things that will make your grandchildren blush.

JOYLETTER

Dear Friend,

As I sit down to pen this joyletter, I'm overwhelmed with Joy that is driven by the profound belief that every woman deserves a place to call her own. A sanctuary where her voice echoes, her stories resonate, and her experiences are honored without judgment and/or reservation. This book is more than just a collection of words bound within pages; it's a testament to the power of sisterhood. It is strength found in shared experiences and the creation of a safe haven for women from all walks of life. It was born out of a deeply felt need to foster a community— a sisterhood where women could feel seen, heard, and understood without shame or need to be perfect.

I embarked on this journey not merely as an author but as a facilitator. One who seeks to cultivate connections among women, weaving threads of understanding and empathy through the tales and wisdom shared within these pages. It is my fervent hope that as you turned those pages, you discovered echoes of your own experiences and found solace in knowing you are not alone, taking comfort in the unity of our collective stories.

May this book catalyze conversations. Conversations that transcend boundaries, break silences, and pave the way for a future where every woman feels empowered, supported, and carefree. It's an invitation to walk together, to listen, to learn, and to uplift one another, devoid of jealousy and shame. As you continue this journey may you move with full understanding that your story matters, your voice is invaluable, and this book is a testament to the resilient, vibrant tapestry that is sisterhood.

Wishing you much JOY,
Alexis M. Bordeaux - Empty Nest Joy

ACKNOWLEDGEMENTS

I express my deepest appreciation to my family, your unwavering support and patience have sustained me through the highs and lows of this creative journey.

Sincere thanks to my mentor and fairy godmother, Linda T., whose wisdom, guidance, and constructive feedback shaped the direction of this book; for you, I am eternally grateful.

I am forever indebted to dear friends, both near and far, who generously shared their stories during interviews and countless dinners and dessert runs. Your willingness to share your stories enriched the content of this book and broadened my perspective on finding joy in midlife.

Lastly, I want to express immense gratitude to my readers and those who have followed me on social media since the beginning of Empty Nest Joy; your interest in this book and your engagement with its ideas gave purpose to the countless hours poured into its creation. It is my hope that these pages inspire, inform, and provide you with a meaningful experience.

With sincere gratitude,
Alexis M. Bordeaux - Empty Nest Joy

Discussion Questions for
Empty Nest Joy
Tangible Tips for Finding Joy After Drop-off

Topics and questions for discussion

1. Which story shared in the book resembles your upbringing?

2. **How has the anti-aging movement impacted your view of aging?**

3. How do you feel about the term aging gracefully? Do you use it to describe your aging process?

4. **If you could visit one place or time in the book, which would it be?**

5. If you could sit for a chat with any of the ladies from the book, who would it be?

6. **What are your thoughts on Evie's belief that she had a hand in not having children?**

7. Which mother/child relationship stood out most to you? And why?

8. **What do you think happened to Camille? Do you think she stayed in Portugal?**

9. How have your cultural beliefs impacted your understanding of aging?

10. **Do you feel comfortable verbalizing moments where you don't feel comfortable in your aging body? Why/why not?**

11. Which of the ladies would fit perfectly in your friend group?

12. **If you were asked to tell the story of your own life, which chapter would be your favorite to share?**

13. Which would be most challenging for you, caring for a previously abusive parent or letting them fend for themselves?

14. **If you could give advice to one character in the book, who would it be, and what would you say?**

15. How accurate were the descriptions of Baby Boomers and Generation X, and can you relate to the characteristics shared in the book?

16. **Would you consider building a home to retire with your close girlfriends?**

17. What are your thoughts on body neutrality vs. body positivity?

18. **Do you consider talks of menopause to be private matters?**

19. Who in the book reminds you of someone in real life? How so?

20. **How is your approach to aging different from that of older women in your family?**

Alexis M. Bordeaux is the creator and chief
nester at Empty Nest Joy. An online resource for all things
Generation X, navigating midlife and thriving in your
empty nest years. When she's not writing or spending
time with family and friends, she can be found people-
watching in her adopted city of Amsterdam, the
Netherlands.

Empty Nest Joy: A Guided Journal for Redefining Your Why

EMPTY NEST JOY

Introducing our companion journal for "Empty Nest Joy:
Tangible Tips for Finding Joy After Drop-off." This 300-page
journal is explicitly designed for empty nesters embarking on
this transformative journey. Our journal is your trusted
companion as you navigate the uncharted waters of this new
season of life.

Packed with insightful prompts, reflective exercises, and
empowering affirmations, this journal is your guide to
rediscovering your purpose and finding fulfillment beyond the
empty nest. Whether seeking clarity on your passions,
redefining your goals, or embracing newfound freedom, our
journal provides the tools you need to thrive in this next
chapter.

www.ingramcontent.com/pod-product-compliance
Lightning Source LLC
Chambersburg PA
CBHW030411130626
46549CB00004B/1719

* 9 7 9 8 2 1 8 3 5 0 0 0 0 *